Hands-On Q-Learning with Python

Practical Q-learning with OpenAI Gym, Keras, and TensorFlow

Nazia Habib

BIRMINGHAM - MUMBAI

Hands-On Q-Learning with Python

Copyright © 2019 Packt Publishing

Commissioning Editor: Pavan Ramchandani
Acquisition Editor: Rohit Rajkumar
Content Development Editor: Nithin George Varghese
Technical Editor: Rutuja Patade
Copy Editor: Safis Editing
Project Coordinator: Nusaiba Ansari
Proofreader: Safis Editing
Indexer: Rekha Nair
Graphics: Tom Scaria
Production Coordinator: Alishon Mendonsa

First published: April 2019

Production reference: 1160419

Published by Packt Publishing Ltd.
Livery Place
35 Livery Street
Birmingham
B3 2PB, UK.

ISBN 978-1-78934-580-3

www.packtpub.com

`mapt.io`

Mapt is an online digital library that gives you full access to over 5,000 books and videos, as well as industry leading tools to help you plan your personal development and advance your career. For more information, please visit our website.

Why subscribe?

- Spend less time learning and more time coding with practical eBooks and Videos from over 4,000 industry professionals

- Improve your learning with Skill Plans built especially for you

- Get a free eBook or video every month

- Mapt is fully searchable

- Copy and paste, print, and bookmark content

Packt.com

Did you know that Packt offers eBook versions of every book published, with PDF and ePub files available? You can upgrade to the eBook version at `www.packt.com` and as a print book customer, you are entitled to a discount on the eBook copy. Get in touch with us at `customercare@packtpub.com` for more details.

At `www.packt.com`, you can also read a collection of free technical articles, sign up for a range of free newsletters, and receive exclusive discounts and offers on Packt books and eBooks.

Contributors

About the author

Nazia Habib is a data scientist who has worked in a variety of industries to generate predictive analytics solutions for diverse groups of stakeholders. She is an expert in building solutions to optimization problems under conditions of uncertainty.

Her projects range from predicting user behavior and engagement with social media apps to designing adaptive testing software. Her ongoing specialization is in designing custom reinforcement learning algorithms for modeling control problems with limited inputs that converge to optimal solutions.

About the reviewers

Sujit Pal is a technology research director at Elsevier Labs, an advanced technology group within the Reed-Elsevier Group. His areas of interest include semantic search, natural language processing, machine learning, and deep learning. At Elsevier, he has worked on several initiatives involving search quality measurement and improvement, image classification and duplicate detection, and annotation and ontology development for medical and scientific corpora. He has co-authored a book on deep learning with Antonio Gulli and writes about technology on his blog, Salmon Run.

Praveen Palanisamy works on developing deep **reinforcement Learning** (**RL**)-based agents to solve tasks that require intelligence. He is currently working as an AI researcher at General Motors' R&D, where he develops Deep RL-based solutions for autonomous driving. He is the inventor of more than 18 patents (pending in > 2 countries) on learning methods for autonomous driving. He is the author of *Hands-On Intelligent Agents with OpenAI Gym*, which provides a step-by-step guide to develop Deep RL agents to solve complex problems. He received his masters degree from the Robotics Institute, School of Computer Science, at Carnegie Mellon University, where he developed deep learning algorithms for perception and planning in mobile robots.

Packt is searching for authors like you

If you're interested in becoming an author for Packt, please visit `authors.packtpub.com` and apply today. We have worked with thousands of developers and tech professionals, just like you, to help them share their insight with the global tech community. You can make a general application, apply for a specific hot topic that we are recruiting an author for, or submit your own idea.

Table of Contents

Preface   1

Section 1: Q-Learning: A Roadmap

Chapter 1: Brushing Up on Reinforcement Learning Concepts   9
  What is RL?   9
    States and actions   11
    The decision-making process   13
    RL, supervised learning, and unsupervised learning   14
  States, actions, and rewards   16
    States   16
    Actions and rewards   18
    Bellman equations   20
  Key concepts in RL   21
    Value-based versus policy-based iteration   21
    Q-learning hyperparameters – alpha, gamma, and epsilon   22
    Alpha – deterministic versus stochastic environments   22
    Gamma – current versus future rewards   23
    Epsilon – exploration versus exploitation   24
    Decaying epsilon   24
  SARSA versus Q-learning – on-policy or off?   26
    SARSA and the cliff-walking problem   27
    When to choose SARSA over Q-learning   28
  Summary   29
  Questions   29

Chapter 2: Getting Started with the Q-Learning Algorithm   31
  Technical requirements   32
  Demystifying MDPs   32
    Control processes   32
    Markov chains   34
    The Markov property   36
    MDPs and state-action diagrams   38
    Solving MDPs with RL   40
  Your Q-learning agent in its environment   41
    Solving the optimization problem   42
    States and actions in Taxi-v2   42
  Fine-tuning your model – learning, discount, and exploration rates   45
    Decaying epsilon   45
    Decaying alpha   46

Decaying gamma 46
MABP – a classic exploration versus exploitation problem 47
Setting up a bandit problem 47
Bandit optimization strategies 49
Other applications for bandit problems 50
Optimal versus safe paths – revisiting SARSA 51
Summary 52
Questions 53

Chapter 3: Setting Up Your First Environment with OpenAI Gym 55
Technical requirements 56
Getting started with OpenAI Gym 56
What is Gym? 56
Setting up Gym 58
Gym environments 58
Setting up an environment 59
Exploring the Taxi-v2 environment 62
The state space and valid actions 63
Choosing an action manually 63
Setting a state manually 65
Creating a baseline agent 66
Stepping through actions 66
Creating a task loop 68
Baseline models in Q-learning and machine learning research 71
Summary 72
Questions 72

Chapter 4: Teaching a Smartcab to Drive Using Q-Learning 73
Technical requirements 74
Getting to know your learning agent 74
Implementing your agent 76
The value function – calculating the Q-value of a state-action pair 79
Implementing Bellman equations 79
The learning parameters – alpha, gamma, and epsilon 84
Adding an updated alpha value 85
Adding an updated epsilon value 86
Model-tuning and tracking your agent's long-term performance 88
Comparing your models and statistical performance measures 88
Training your models 90
Decaying epsilon 92
Hyperparameter tuning 93
Summary 94
Questions 94

Section 2: Building and Optimizing Q-Learning Agents

Chapter 5: Building Q-Networks with TensorFlow 99
Technical requirements 100
A brief overview of neural networks 100
Extensional versus intensional definitions 101
Taking a closer look 101
Input, hidden, and output layers 102
Perceptron functions 102
ReLU functions 105
Implementing a neural network with NumPy 106
Feedforward 107
Backpropagation 107
Neural networks and Q-learning 109
Policy agents versus value agents 109
Building your first Q-network 110
Defining the network 111
Training the network 112
Summary 114
Questions 115
Further reading 115

Chapter 6: Digging Deeper into Deep Q-Networks with Keras and TensorFlow 117
Technical requirements 118
Introducing CartPole-v1 118
More about CartPole states and actions 120
Getting started with the CartPole task 121
Building a DQN to solve the CartPole problem 122
Gamma 124
Alpha 124
Epsilon 124
Building a DQN class 125
Choosing actions with epsilon-greedy 125
Updating the Q-values 126
Running the task loop 127
Testing and results 129
Adding in experience replay 130
About experience replay 130
Implementation 131
Experience replay results 132
Building further on DQNs 133
Calculating DQN loss 133

Fixed Q-targets   134
Double-deep Q-networks   134
Dueling deep Q-networks   134
Summary   136
Questions   136
Further reading   136

Section 3: Advanced Q-Learning Challenges with Keras, TensorFlow, and OpenAI Gym

Chapter 7: Decoupling Exploration and Exploitation in Multi-Armed Bandits   139
Technical requirements   139
Probability distributions and ongoing knowledge   140
Iterative probability distributions   141
Revisiting a simple bandit problem   142
A sample two-armed bandit iteration   143
Multi-armed bandit strategy overview   144
Greedy strategy   144
Epsilon-greedy strategy   145
Upper confidence bound   146
Bandit regret   147
Utility functions and optimal decisions   147
Contextual bandits and state diagrams   148
Thompson sampling and the Bayesian control rule   149
Thompson sampling   149
Bayesian control rule   151
Solving a multi-armed bandit problem in Python – user advertisement clicks   152
Epsilon-greedy selection   154
Multi-armed bandits in experimental design   155
The testing process   156
Bandits with knapsacks – more multi-armed bandit applications   157
Summary   158
Questions   158
Further reading   159

Chapter 8: Further Q-Learning Research and Future Projects   161
Google's DeepMind and the future of Q-learning   161
OpenAI Gym and RL research   162
The standardization of RL research practice with Gym   164
Tracking your scores with the Gym leaderboard   164
More OpenAI Gym environments   164
Pendulum   165
Acrobot   166

MountainCar   167
Continuous control tasks – MuJoCo   168
Continuous control tasks – Box2D   170
Robotics research and development   171
Algorithms   172
Toy text   173
Contextual bandits and probability distributions   175
Probability and intelligence   175
Updating probability distributions   176
State spaces   178
A/B testing versus multi-armed bandit testing   179
Testing methodologies   179
Summary   181
Questions   181
Further reading   182
Assessments   183
Other Books You May Enjoy   191
Index   195

Preface

This book will introduce the Q-learning algorithm using OpenAI Gym, TensorFlow, and Keras in a Python programming environment.

We will start by writing model-free Q-learning implementations to solve toy text problems and then learn how to use Q-networks and deep Q-networks to solve more complex problems. We will also learn how to tune and optimize Q-networks and their hyperparameters. Finally, we will discuss how Q-learning and related algorithms are used in real-world applications, such as scientific research and experimental design.

Use cases will include OpenAI Gym's Taxi and CartPole environments.

Who this book is for

Readers of this book should have a Python 3.5+ development environment available and be comfortable with programming Python at least to an intermediate level.

If you are a data science or machine learning practitioner, you have the ideal background for approaching the problems encountered in this book. To be able to work through the material, you should have some knowledge of descriptive statistics, linear algebra, and probability theory, as well as Python programming.

What this book covers

Chapter 1, *Brushing Up on Reinforcement Learning Concepts*, covers the building-block concepts of agents, environments, states, actions, rewards, policies, and values. The reader will be introduced to stochastic and deterministic environments, learning rates, and exploration versus exploitation.

Chapter 2, *Getting Started with the Q-Learning Algorithm*, covers in great depth how a Markov decision process works and the way a Q-learning algorithm is designed to solve it. We will discuss what kinds of problems can and can't be solved with a model-free algorithm, as well as the types of problems that Q-learning is especially well suited to.

Chapter 3, *Setting Up Your First Environment with OpenAI Gym*, covers using OpenAI Gym to set up environments and begin building our first randomly-acting RL agent. We will set up a sample environment and become familiar with the basic tools and functionality of Gym.

Chapter 4, *Teaching a Smartcab to Drive Using Q-Learning*, covers building your first model-free Q-learning agent in OpenAI Gym, a simulation of a self-driving vehicle dropping a passenger off at a destination. You will build and test your agent's decision-making algorithm and observe the conditions under which its value function converges.

Chapter 5, *Building Q-Networks with TensorFlow*, covers learning how to use a neural network with a Q-learning algorithm to solve an environment, such as in cases where the state space becomes too large to be modeled with a Q-table. We will learn the challenges of solving a reinforcement learning task in an environment with sparse data.

Chapter 6, *Digging Deeper into Deep Q-Networks with Keras and TensorFlow*, explains how to build more advanced Q-learning models by combining Q-learning with deep learning and giving the agent an existing model of a problem to work from. This section contains an implementation for a solution to the CartPole problem from OpenAI Gym.

Chapter 7, *Decoupling Exploration and Exploitation in Multi-Armed Bandits*, covers the problem of multi-armed bandits and extends the concept of exploration versus exploitation. We will explore well-known examples of these problems and talk about why bandit problems are scientifically interesting.

Chapter 8, *Further Q-Learning Research and Future Projects*, covers a wide range of problems to consider for future projects in Q-learning. You will leave the chapter with a wealth of knowledge on how to continue your research as an RL practitioner.

To get the most out of this book

You should have a Python development environment available and be comfortable with programming Python at least to an intermediate level.

You should have some knowledge of descriptive statistics, linear algebra, and probability theory. If you are a data science or machine learning practitioner, you have the ideal background for approaching the problems in this book.

You will need to be able to run Python 3.5+ in order to use OpenAI Gym. You can either install Gym from pip or clone the Gym repository itself.

Download the example code files

You can download the example code files for this book from your account at www.packt.com. If you purchased this book elsewhere, you can visit www.packt.com/support and register to have the files emailed directly to you.

You can download the code files by following these steps:

1. Log in or register at www.packt.com.
2. Select the **SUPPORT** tab.
3. Click on **Code Downloads & Errata**.
4. Enter the name of the book in the **Search** box and follow the onscreen instructions.

Once the file is downloaded, please make sure that you unzip or extract the folder using the latest version of:

- WinRAR/7-Zip for Windows
- Zipeg/iZip/UnRarX for Mac
- 7-Zip/PeaZip for Linux

The code bundle for the book is also hosted on GitHub at https://github.com/PacktPublishing/Hands-On-Q-Learning-with-Python. In case there's an update to the code, it will be updated on the existing GitHub repository.

We also have other code bundles from our rich catalog of books and videos available at https://github.com/PacktPublishing/. Check them out!

Download the color images

We also provide a PDF file that has color images of the screenshots/diagrams used in this book. You can download it here: https://www.packtpub.com/sites/default/files/downloads/9781789345803_ColorImages.pdf.

Conventions used

There are a number of text conventions used throughout this book.

CodeInText: Indicates code words in text, database table names, folder names, filenames, file extensions, pathnames, dummy URLs, user input, and Twitter handles. Here is an example: "This is an assignment where we are setting the value of Q[state, action]."

A block of code is set as follows:

```
import gym
import numpy as np
env = gym.make('Taxi-v2')
state = env.reset()
```

When we wish to draw your attention to a particular part of a code block, the relevant lines or items are set in bold:

```
import gym
import numpy as np
env = gym.make('Taxi-v2')
state = env.reset()
```

Any command-line input or output is written as follows:

```
pip install gym
```

Bold: Indicates a new term, an important word, or words that you see on screen. For example: "The two major model-free RL algorithms are called **Q-learning** and **State-Action-Reward-State-Action (SARSA)**."

 Warnings or important notes appear like this.

 Tips and tricks appear like this.

Get in touch

Feedback from our readers is always welcome.

General feedback: If you have questions about any aspect of this book, mention the book title in the subject of your message and email us at customercare@packtpub.com.

Errata: Although we have taken every care to ensure the accuracy of our content, mistakes do happen. If you have found a mistake in this book, we would be grateful if you would report this to us. Please visit www.packt.com/submit-errata, selecting your book, clicking on the Errata Submission Form link, and entering the details.

Piracy: If you come across any illegal copies of our works in any form on the internet, we would be grateful if you would provide us with the location address or website name. Please contact us at copyright@packt.com with a link to the material.

If you are interested in becoming an author: If there is a topic that you have expertise in, and you are interested in either writing or contributing to a book, please visit `authors.packtpub.com`.

Reviews

Please leave a review. Once you have read and used this book, why not leave a review on the site that you purchased it from? Potential readers can then see and use your unbiased opinion to make purchase decisions, we at Packt can understand what you think about our products, and our authors can see your feedback on their book. Thank you!

For more information about Packt, please visit `packt.com`.

Section 1: Q-Learning: A Roadmap

This section will introduces the reader to reinforcement learning and Q-learning, and the types of problem that can be solved with both. Readers will become familiar with OpenAI Gym as a tool for creating Q-learning projects and will build their first model-free Q-learning agent.

The following chapters are included in this section:

- Chapter 1, *Brushing Up on Reinforcement Learning Concepts*
- Chapter 2, *Getting Started with the Q-Learning Algorithm*
- Chapter 3, *Setting Up Your First Environment with OpenAI Gym*
- Chapter 4, *Teaching a Smartcab to Drive Using Q-Learning*

Brushing Up on Reinforcement Learning Concepts

1

In this book, you will learn the fundamentals of Q-learning, a branch of **reinforcement learning** (**RL**), and how to apply them to challenging real-world optimization problems. You'll design software that dynamically writes itself, modifies itself, and improves its own performance in real time.

In doing so, you will build self-learning intelligent agents that start with no knowledge of how to solve a problem and independently find optimal solutions to that problem through observation, trial and error, and memory.

RL is one of the most exciting branches of **artificial intelligence** (**AI**) and powers some of its most visible successes, from recommendation systems that learn from user behavior to game-playing machines that can beat any human being at chess or Go.

Q-learning is one of the easiest versions of RL to get started with, and mastering it will give you a solid foundation in your knowledge and practice of RL. Whether you work as a data scientist, machine learning engineer, or other practitioner in the data or AI space, you will find plenty of useful and practical resources to get you started.

We will cover the following topics in this introductory chapter:

- Reviewing RL and the differences between reward-based learning and other types of machine learning
- Learning what states are and what it means to take an action and receive a reward
- Understanding how RL agents make decisions based on policies and future rewards
- Discovering the two major types of model-free RL and diving deeper into Q-learning

What is RL?

An RL agent is an optimization process that learns from experience, using data from its environment that it has collected through its own observations. It starts out knowing nothing about a task explicitly, learns by trial and error about what happens when it makes decisions, keeps track of successful decisions, and makes those same decisions under the same circumstances in the future.

In fields other than AI, RL is also referred to as dynamic programming. It takes much of its basic operating structure from behavioral psychology, and many of its mathematical constructs such as utility functions are taken from fields such as economics and game theory.

Let's get familiar with some key concepts in RL:

- **Agent**: This is the decision-making entity.
- **Environment**: This is the world in which the agent operates, such as a game to win or task to accomplish.
- **State**: This is where the agent is in its environment. When you define the states that an agent can be in, think about what it needs to know about its environment. For example, a self-driving car will need to know whether the next traffic light is red or green and whether there are pedestrians in the crosswalk; these are defined as state variables.
- **Action**: This is the next move that the agent chooses to take.
- **Reward**: This is the feedback that the agent gets from the environment for taking that action.
- **Policy**: This is a function to map the agent's states to its actions. For your first RL agent, this will be as simple as a lookup table, called the Q-table. It will operate as your agent's brain.
- **Value**: This is the **future reward** that an agent would receive by taking an action based on the future actions it could take. This is separate from the immediate reward it will get from taking that action (the value is also commonly called the **utility**).

The first type of RL agent that you will create is a **model-free** agent. A model-free RL agent does not know anything about a state that it has not seen, and so will not be able to estimate the value of the reward that it will receive from an unknown state. In other words, it cannot generalize about its environment. We will explore the differences between model-free learning and model-based learning in greater depth later in the book.

The two major model-free RL algorithms are called **Q-learning** and **state-action-reward-state-action** (**SARSA**). The algorithm that we will use throughout the book is Q-learning.

As we will see in the *SARSA versus Q-learning – on-policy or off?* section comparing the two algorithms, Q-learning can be treated as a variant of SARSA. We choose to use Q-learning as our introductory RL algorithm because it is relatively simple and straightforward to learn. As we build on and increase our RL skills, we can branch out into other algorithms that may be more complicated to learn, but they will give us better results.

States and actions

When first launched, your agent knows nothing about its environment and takes purely random actions.

As an example, suppose that a hypothetical self-driving car powered by a Q-learning algorithm notices that it's reached a red light, but it doesn't know that it's supposed to stop. It moves one block forward and receives a large penalty.

The car makes note of that penalty in the Q-table. The next time it encounters a red light, it looks at the Q-table when deciding what to do, and because the move-forward action in the state where it is stopped at a red light now has a lower reward value than any other action, it is less likely to decide to run the red light again.

Likewise, when it takes a correct action, such as stopping at a red light or safely moving closer to the destination, it gets a reward. Thus, it remembers that taking that action in that state led to a reward, and it becomes more likely to take that action again next time.

While a self-driving car in the real world will, of course, not be expected to teach itself what red lights mean, the driving problem is a popular learning simulation (and one that we'll be implementing in this book) because it's straightforward and easy to model as a state-action function (also called a **finite state machine**).The following is a sample finite state machine:

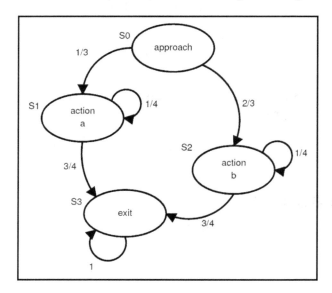

When we model a state-action function for any system, we decide the variables that we want to keep track of, and this lets us determine how many states the system can be in.

For example, a state variable for a vehicle might include information about what intersection the car is located at, whether the traffic light is red or green, and whether there are other cars around. Because we're keeping track of multiple variables, we might represent this as a vector.

The possible actions for a self-driving vehicle agent can be: move forward one block, turn left, turn right, and stop and wait – and these actions are mapped to the appropriate values of the state variable.

Recall that an agent's state-action function is called its **policy**. A policy can be either simple and straightforward or complex and difficult to enumerate, depending on the problem itself and the number of states and actions.

In the model-free version of Q-learning, it's important to note that we do not learn an agent's policy explicitly. We only update the output values that we see as a result of that policy, which we are mapping to the state-action inputs. This is why we refer to model-free Q-learning as a **value-based** algorithm as opposed to a **policy-based** algorithm.

The decision-making process

A learning agent's high-level algorithm looks like the following:

1. Take note of what state you're in.
2. Take an action based on your policy and receive a reward.
3. Take note of the reward you received by taking that action in that state.

We can express this mathematically using a **Markov decision process (MDP)**. We'll discuss MDPs in more detail throughout the book. For now, we need to be aware that an MDP describes an environment for RL in which the current state tells us everything we need to know about future states.

What this means, in short, is that if we know the current state of the environment in an MDP, we don't need to know anything about any past states in order to determine what future states will be, or decide what actions to take in this current state. The following diagram shows an illustration of an MDP:

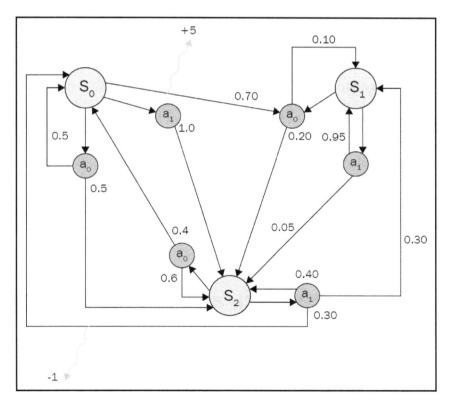

The preceding diagram shows a stochastic MDP with three states: S_0, S_1, and S_2. When we are in state S_0, we can take either action a_0 or action a_1. If we take action a_0, there is a 50% chance that we will end up in state S_2 and a 50% chance we will end up back in state S_0. If we take action a_1, there is a 100% chance we will end up in state S_2, and so on.

The different actions we choose can have different probable outcomes that we will determine over time through observation. In the MDPs that we work with, there will be rewards associated with each step, and our goal will be to maximize the rewards we receive by knowing the outcomes of each action we choose to take. The more we learn about this environment over time, the better the position we are in to take high-reward actions we've seen before.

Recall that because this environment is stochastic, we do not always end up in the same state based on each action we take. If the environment had been deterministic, we would always end up in the same state after each action we took.

Stochastic environments are also referred to as probabilistic. That is, they incorporate inherent randomness so that the same parameter values and initial conditions can lead to different outcomes. Virtually all natural processes in the real world are stochastic to some degree and involve some level of randomness.

As we'll discuss later in the book, sources of randomness and probability can be modeled on our own uncertainty about an environment rather than on a property that is inherent to the environment itself. In other words, an event will either happen or not happen. Probability and randomness are not properties inherent to that event; they exist only in our perception of the event. In this model, therefore, probability is inherently subjective.

This formulation of stochastic processes is a foundational concept of Bayesian reasoning and the source of many useful mathematical models of agency that are driven by belief and the continual updating of knowledge based on observation. We'll dive deeper into these topics in `Chapter 8`, *Further Q-Learning Research and Future Projects*, when we talk about multi-armed bandits and optimization processes, but they are useful to investigate in other contexts as well.

RL, supervised learning, and unsupervised learning

What is the difference between RL, supervised learning, and unsupervised learning? Well, all of them involve developing rules about an unknown environment using labeled or unlabeled data. The following is a simple diagram charting the different terms:

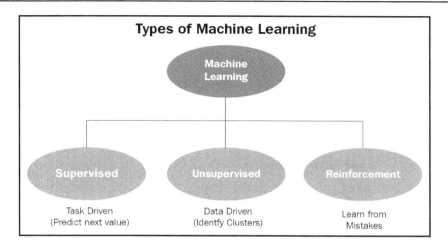

Take a look at the following definitions of each term:

- **Supervised learning** feeds labeled training data into an algorithm, trains the algorithm on that data, generates predictions for unlabeled testing data, and then compares the predictions of the model to the actual labels. The goal of supervised learning is to generate class labels for unseen data or to predict unseen numerical values using regression.
- **Unsupervised learning** looks for similarities between different observations of unlabeled data. An unsupervised learning algorithm looks for observations that fit together along axes of similarity. The goal of unsupervised learning is to group together similar observations based on relevant criteria.
- **RL** seeks to optimize a variable under a set of constraints. An RL algorithm, called an agent, is seeking an optimal path to a goal. Therefore, the goal of RL is to find a set of actions, mapped to a set of states, that leads us to the best possible outcome in a situation that we have limited information about.

The primary difference between these three learning methods is in the type of question being asked:

- Supervised learning works well for classification and regression problems (for example, whether a customer will buy a product or how much they might spend)
- Unsupervised learning works well for problems dealing with association (for example, what products customers might buy together) and anomaly detection
- RL works best when there is a specific value to be optimized and a function that can be discovered within a problem to optimize it (for example, how can we maximize the number of times a user will click on links or download apps based on the advertisements that we show them)

Note that this list of uses for each method is not exhaustive; we are only presenting well-known examples of the type of problem each method tends to work well for.

There are many other examples of questions that we might ask and other machine learning algorithms that we might use to solve them, but understanding the broad similarities and differences between these three major types will be useful for us going forward.

States, actions, and rewards

What does it mean to be in a state, to take an action, or to receive a reward? These are the most important concepts for us to understand intuitively, so let's dig deeper into them. The following diagram depicts the agent-environment interaction in an MDP:

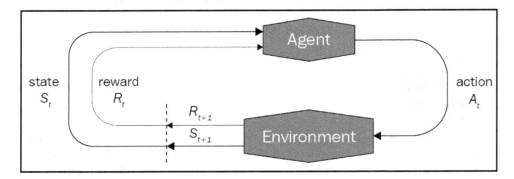

The agent interacts with the environment through actions, and it receives rewards and state information from the environment. In other words, the states and rewards are feedback from the environment, and the actions are inputs to the environment from the agent.

Going back to our simple driving simulator example, our agent might be moving or stopped at a red light, turning left or right, or heading straight. There might be other cars in the intersection, or there might not be. Our distance from the destination will be X units.

States

Whatever we need to know about our environment is stored as part of our state, which can be represented as a vector of the variables that we care about:

- The location (x and y coordinates)
- The direction

- The color of light (red or green)
- The other cars present (for example, one binary flag for each spot a car might be in)
- The distance from the destination

The following screenshot is from the game Pac-Man:

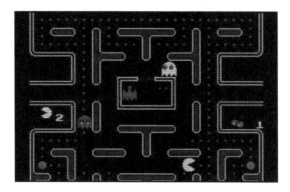

Taking Pac-Man as another example, we can use a state vector to represent the variables that we want to keep track of—such as the location of the dots left in the maze, where the Pac-Man character currently is and what direction it is moving in, the location and direction of each ghost, and whether the ghosts can be eaten or not.

We can represent any variables in our state vector that we think are important to our knowledge of the game. At any point in time, our state vector should represent for us the things that we want to know about our environment.

Ideally, we should be able to look at our state vector and have all the information we need to optimally determine what action we need to take. A well-designed state space is key to an effective RL solution.

However, we can quickly see that the number of states in an environment depends on the variables that we choose to keep track of. In other words, it is arbitrary to some respect. Not all algorithm designers will represent the same environment using the same state space. One thing we notice (as developers and researchers) is that even a small change in the way state spaces are represented in an environment can cause a huge difference in the difficulty level of a problem.

When we use a standardized packaged environment such as the ones we'll be working with in OpenAI Gym, the state space (also called an observation space) will be determined for us. We'll also have a predetermined action space and reward structure.

One good reason to use a standardized environment such as the one offered by OpenAI Gym is that it allows you to compare the performance of your RL algorithms to the work of others. Having a level playing field for the state space allows us to meaningfully compare RL algorithms to each other in a way we otherwise could not.

Actions and rewards

An action is any decision that we make from a state. The state that we are in determines the actions we can take. If we are in a maze and to the right of a wall, we can't turn left, but in other locations, we can turn left. Turning left may or may not be in the list of possible actions that we can take in any particular state.

A reward is the outcome we receive for making a decision in an environment. Our Q-learning agent will keep track of the rewards it receives and will try to maximize the future rewards that it expects to receive with each action it takes.

The reward function for a driving simulator can be something straightforward, such as the following:

- +1 for moving one block
- +10 for making the correct move that will get you closer to the destination
- +100 for reaching the destination
- -20 for violating traffic laws
- -50 for hitting another vehicle

Every action we take leads to a reward, and each reward is noted by the learning agent as it explores its environment and learns what the best actions are to take in each state. For a Q-learning agent, these rewards are stored in a Q-table, which is a simple lookup table mapping states to actions. We will be creating a Q-table as part of our first project, which will be the OpenAI Gym Taxi-v2 environment shown here. The following ASCII screenshot shows a representation of the environment:

```
import gym
env = gym.make "Taxi-v2"
env.render()

+---------+
|R: | : :G|
| : : : : |
| : : : : |
| | : | : |
|Y| : |B: |
+---------+
```

The **Taxi-v2** environment simulates a taxicab driving around a small grid, picking up passengers and dropping them off at the correct locations. Retrieving the action space and state space from our taxi environment lets us know how many discrete actions and states we have:

```
print("Action Space {}".format(env.action_space))
print("State Space {}".format(env.observation_space))

Action Space Discrete(6)
State Space Discrete(500)
```

The following is a representation of a Q-table for **Taxi-v2**. Note that it lists 500 states and 6 actions (**South**, **North**, **East**, **West**, **Pickup**, and **Dropoff**):

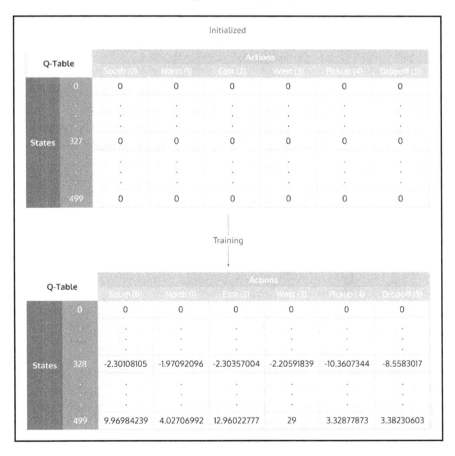

When the Q-table is initialized, each state-action pair has a value of zero, because the agent has not seen any rewards yet and has not set a value for any action. Once it explores its environment, it starts to fill in values for each state-action pair and to use those values to decide what actions to take the next time it is in those states.

If we, as the agent, are in a particular state, such as state 300, and have 6 possible actions to choose from (as in the taxi example), depending on how much exploration we have done and how many iterations we have gone through, each action will have a different value. Let's say that **East** has a value of 2, **Pickup** has a value of 9, and all other actions have a value of 0.

Pickup is, therefore, the highest-valued action, and when we plug it into our `argmax` function, we have a high probability of choosing **Pickup** as our next action, depending on our hyperparameter values. Given that **Pickup** is highly valued at this point above all other actions, it is very likely that it is the correct action to take.

Depending on our agent's policy (that is, the function it uses to choose actions based on states), however, it may or may not actually choose **Pickup**. If it is using an epsilon-greedy strategy, for example, it might choose a random action instead, which could turn out to be completely wrong.

This is important to bear in mind as we choose a decision-making strategy. We do not always want to choose the current highest-valued action, as there may be other higher-valued actions that we haven't discovered yet. This process is called **exploration**, and we'll discuss several methodologies for using it to find optimal reward paths.

Bellman equations

As we mentioned, the Q-table functions as your agent's brain. Everything it has learned about its environment is stored in this table. The function that powers your agent's decisions is called a Bellman equation. There are many different Bellman equations, and we will be using a version of the following equation:

$$newQ(s, a) = Q(s, a) + \alpha[R(s, a) + \gamma[maxQ'(s', a') - Q(s, a)]]$$

Here, *newQ(s,a)* is the new value that we are computing for the state-action pair to enter into the Q-table; *Q(s,a)* is the current state; alpha is the learning rate; *R(s,a)* is the reward for that state-action pair; gamma is the discount rate; and *maxQ(s', a')* is the maximum expected future reward given to the new state (that is, the highest possible reward for all of the actions the agent could take from the new state):

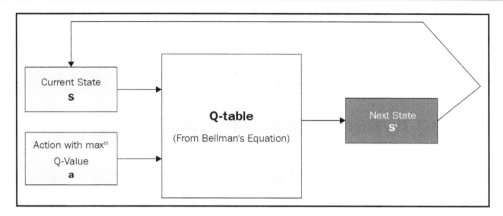

This equation might seem intimidating at first, but it will become much more straightforward once we start translating it into Python code. The `maxQ'(s', a')` term will be implemented with an `argmax` function, which we will discuss in detail. This applies to most of the complex math we will encounter here; once you begin coding, it becomes much simpler and clearer to understand.

Key concepts in RL

Here, we'll go over some of the most important concepts that we'll need to bear in mind throughout our study of RL. We'll focus heavily on topics that are specific to Q-learning, but we'll also explore topics relating to other branches of RL, such as the related algorithm SARSA and policy-based RL algorithms.

Value-based versus policy-based iteration

We'll be using value-based iteration for the projects in this book. The description of the Bellman equation given previously offers a very high-level understanding of how value-based iteration works. The main difference is that in value-based iteration, the agent learns the expected reward value of each state-action pair, and in policy-based iteration, the agent learns the function that maps states to actions.

One simple way to describe this difference is that a value-based agent, when it has mastered its environment, will not explicitly be able to simulate that environment. It will not be able to give an actual function that maps states to actions. A policy-based agent, on the other hand, will be able to give that function.

Note that Q-learning and SARSA are both value-based algorithms. Because we are working with Q-learning in this book, we will not study policy-based iteration in detail here. The main thing to bear in mind about policy-based iteration is that it gives us the ability to learn stochastic policies and it is more useful for working with continuous action spaces.

Q-learning hyperparameters – alpha, gamma, and epsilon

The hyperparameters of your model are the parameters that are external to the model that you will set yourself (think of the k value in an algorithm such as k-nearest neighbors; this is a hyperparameter. You have to set it yourself as there is nothing inherent in the data that determines what k should be).

The three most important hyperparameters for your agent are as follows:

- **Alpha**: The learning rate
- **Gamma**: The discount rate
- **Epsilon**: The exploration rate

Alpha – deterministic versus stochastic environments

Your agent's learning rate alpha ranges from zero to one. Setting the learning rate to zero will cause your agent to learn nothing. All of its exploration of its environment and the rewards it receives will not affect its behavior at all, and it will continue to behave completely randomly.

Setting the learning rate to one will cause your agent to learn policies that are fully specific to a deterministic environment. One important distinction to understand is between **deterministic** and **stochastic** environments and policies.

Briefly, in a deterministic environment, the output is totally determined by the initial conditions and there is no randomness involved. We always take the same action from the same state in a deterministic environment.

In a stochastic environment, there is randomness involved and the decisions that we make are given as probability distributions. In other words, we don't always take the same action from the same state.

Gamma – current versus future rewards

Let's discuss the concept of current rewards versus future rewards. Your agent's discount rate gamma has a value between zero and one, and its function is to discount future rewards against immediate rewards.

Your agent is deciding what action to take based not only on the reward it expects to get for taking that action, but on the future rewards it might be able to get from the state it will be in after taking that action.

One easy way to illustrate discounting rewards is with the following example of a mouse in a maze collecting cheese as rewards and avoiding cats and traps (that is, electric shocks):

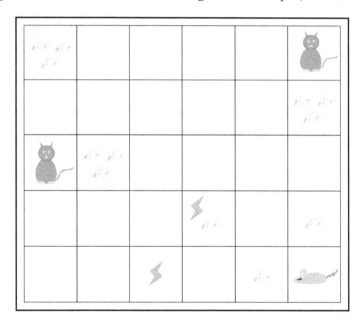

The rewards that are closest to the cats, even though their point values are higher (three versus one), should be discounted if we want to maximize how long the mouse agent lives and how much cheese it can collect. These rewards come with a higher risk of the mouse being killed, so we lower their value accordingly. In other words, collecting the closest cheese should be given a higher priority when the mouse decides what actions to take.

When we discount a future reward, we make it less valuable than an immediate reward (similar to how we take into account the time value of money when making a loan and treat a dollar received today as more valuable than a dollar received a year from now).

The value of gamma that we choose varies according to how highly we value future rewards:

- If we choose a value of zero for gamma, the agent will not care about future rewards at all and will only take current rewards into account
- Choosing a value of one for gamma will make the agent consider future rewards as highly as current rewards

Epsilon – exploration versus exploitation

Your agent's exploration rate epsilon also ranges from zero to one. As the agent explores its environment, it learns that some actions are better to take than others, but what about states and actions that it hasn't seen yet? We don't want it to get stuck on a local maximum, taking the same currently highest-valued actions over and over when there might be better actions it hasn't tried to take yet.

When you set your epsilon value, there will be a probability equal to epsilon that your agent will take a random (exploratory) action, and a probability equal to 1-epsilon that it will take the current highest Q-valued action for its current state. As we step through a full Q-table update example in the *SARSA and the cliff-walking problem* section, we'll see how the value that we choose for epsilon affects the rate at which the Q-table converges and the agent discovers the optimal solution.

As the agent gets more and more familiar with its environment, we want it to start sticking to the high-valued actions it's already discovered and do less exploration of the states it hasn't seen. We achieve this by having epsilon decay over time as the agent learns more about its environment and the Q-table converges on its final optimal values.

There are many different ways to decay epsilon, either by using a constant decay factor or basing the decay factor on some other internal variable. Ideally, we want the epsilon decay function to be directly based on the Q-values that we've already discovered. We'll discuss what this means in the next section.

Decaying epsilon

The more familiar your agent becomes with its environment, the less exploration we want it to do. As it discovers more and more rewards, the odds that it will discover actions with higher reward values than the ones it has already discovered begin to decrease. It should start to increasingly stick with actions it knows are highly-valued and do less and less exploration.

This concept is called exploration versus exploitation. Exploration refers to discovering new states that may be higher-valued than the ones our agent has already seen, and exploitation means visiting the highest-valued states it has seen to benefit from the rewards it already knows it will collect there.

One popular illustration of this problem is the multi-armed bandit. A one-armed bandit is a slot machine, and an *n*-armed bandit is a hypothetical slot machine with *n* arms, each of which has a rigged probability that it will pay out a fixed percentage of the time.

We have a limited amount of money to put into this slot machine. Each arm will either give us a reward or not when we pull it, and each arm has a different probability of giving us a payout on each pull.

We want to maximize our total rewards for the money that we put in. So, which arm should we pull on our next try? Take a look at the following diagram illustrating the state of the multi-armed bandit:

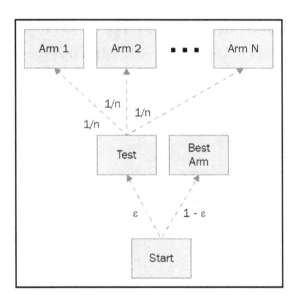

When we first begin to solve this task, we don't know what the true probability is that we'll receive a reward from any of the arms. The only way for us to learn what will happen is to pull the arms and see.

As the agent in this situation, we are learning what our environment is like as we go. When we don't know anything about the arms and their payouts, we want to pull all of the arms until we get a good idea of how often they will pay out. If we learn that one arm pays out more often than others, we want to start pulling that arm more often.

The only way we can have a clear idea of what the true payout probabilities are is by sampling the arms enough, but once we do have a clear signal for those probabilities we should follow it to maximize our total payout. So, how can we devise a strategy to do this?

We will explore solutions to the multi-armed bandit problem in later chapters, but it's important to be able to put it in the context of epsilon decay. This is because epsilon is the value that tells us how often we should explore new actions as opposed to how often we should exploit the knowledge we already have of the actions we've taken; therefore, it's important that the epsilon changes as we progress through an environment.

In the problems that we'll be working on, we'll see that we should be exploring less and exploiting more as we gain more knowledge of our environment, so epsilon should decrease as we progress. We'll discuss well-known strategies for decaying epsilon, or making it decrease, based on the parameters within the problem that we've set.

SARSA versus Q-learning – on-policy or off?

Similar to Q-learning, SARSA is a model-free RL method that does not explicitly learn the agent's policy function.

The primary difference between SARSA and Q-learning is that SARSA is an on-policy method while Q-learning is an off-policy method. The effective difference between the two algorithms happens in the step where the Q-table is updated. Let's discuss what that means with some examples:

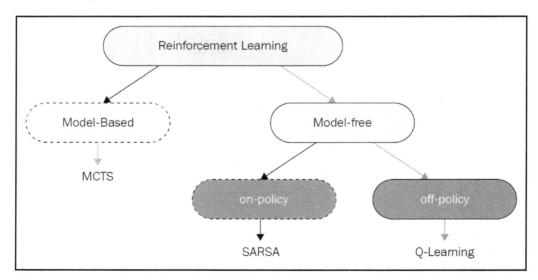

Monte Carlo tree search (**MCTS**) is a type of model-based RL. We won't be discussing it in detail here, but it's useful to explore further as a contrast to model-free RL algorithms. Briefly, in model-based RL, we attempt to explicitly model a value function instead of relying on sampling and observation, so that we don't have to rely as much on trial and error in the learning process.

SARSA and the cliff-walking problem

In Q-learning, the agent starts out in state S, performs action A, sees what the highest possible reward is for taking any action from its new state, T, and updates its value for the state S-action A pair based on this new highest possible value. In SARSA, the agent starts in state S, takes action A and gets a reward, then moves to state T, takes action B and gets a reward, and then goes back to update the value for S-A based on the actual value of the reward it received from taking action B.

A famous illustration of the differences in performance between Q-learning and SARSA is the cliff-walking example from Sutton and Barto's *Reinforcement Learning: An Introduction* (1998):

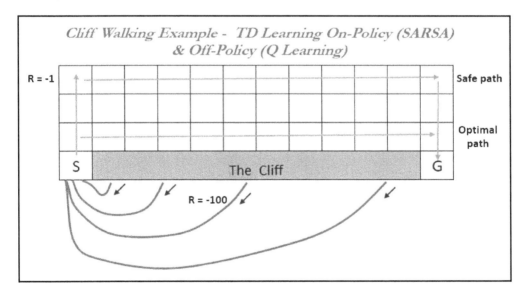

There is a penalty of **-1** for each step that the agent takes, and a penalty of **-100** for falling off the cliff. The optimal path is, therefore, to run exactly along the edge of the cliff and reach the reward as quickly as possible. This minimizes the number of steps the agent takes and maximizes its reward as long as it does not fall into the cliff at any point.

Q-learning takes the optimal path in this example, while SARSA takes the safe path. The result is that there is a nonzero risk (with an epsilon-greedy or other exploration-based policy) that at any point a Q-learning agent will fall off the cliff as a result of choosing exploration.

SARSA, unlike Q-learning, looks ahead to the next action to see what the agent will actually do at the next step and updates the Q-value of its current state-action pair accordingly. For this reason, it learns that the agent might fall into the cliff and that this would lead to a large negative reward, so it lowers the Q-values of those state-action pairs accordingly.

The result is that Q-learning assumes that the agent is following the best possible policy without attempting to resolve what that policy actually is, while SARSA takes into account the agent's actual policy (that is, what it ends up doing when it moves to the next state as opposed to the best possible thing it could be assumed to do).

When to choose SARSA over Q-learning

As mentioned earlier, Q-learning and SARSA are very similar algorithms, and in fact, Q-learning is sometimes called SARSA-max. When the agent's policy is simply the greedy one (that is, it chooses the highest-valued action from the next state no matter what), Q-learning and SARSA will produce the same results.

In practice, we will not be using a simple greedy strategy and will instead choose something such as epsilon-greedy, where some of the actions are chosen at random. We will explore this in more depth when we discuss epsilon decay strategies further.

We can, therefore, think of SARSA as a more general version of Q-learning. The algorithms are very similar, and in practice, modifying a Q-learning implementation to SARSA involves nothing more than changing the update method for the Q-values. As we've seen, however, the difference in performance can be profound.

In many problems, SARSA will perform better than Q-learning, especially when there is a good chance that the agent will choose to take a random suboptimal action in the next step, as we explored in the cliff-walking example. In this case, Q-learning's assumption that the agent is following the optimal policy may be far enough from true that SARSA will converge faster and with fewer errors.

Summary

RL is one of the most exciting and fastest-growing branches of machine learning, with the greatest potential to create powerful optimization solutions to wide-ranging computing problems. As we have seen, Q-learning is one of the most accessible branches of RL and will provide a beginning RL practitioner and experienced programmer a strong foundation for developing solutions to both straightforward and complex optimization problems.

In the next chapter, we'll learn about Q-learning in detail, as well as about the learning agent that we'll be training to solve our Q-learning task. We'll discuss how Q-learning solves MDPs using a state-action model and how to apply that to our programming task.

Questions

1. What is the difference between a reward and a value?
2. What is a hyperparameter? Give an example of a hyperparameter other than the ones discussed in this chapter.
3. Why will a Q-learning agent not choose the highest Q-valued action for its current state?
4. Explain one benefit of a decaying gamma.
5. Describe in one or two sentences the difference between the decision-making strategies of SARSA and Q-learning.
6. What kind of policy does Q-learning implicitly assume the agent is following?
7. Under what circumstances will SARSA and Q-learning produce the same results?

Getting Started with the Q-Learning Algorithm

2

Q-learning is an algorithm that is designed to solve a control problem called a **Markov decision process** (**MDP**). We will go over what MDPs are in detail, how they work, and how Q-learning is designed to solve them. We will explore some classic **reinforcement learning** (**RL**) problems and learn how to develop solutions using Q-learning.

We will cover the following topics in this chapter:

- Understanding what an MDP is and how Q-learning is designed to solve an MDP
- Learning how to define the states an agent can be in, and the actions it can take from those states in the context of the OpenAI Gym Taxi-v2 environment that we will be using for our first project
- Becoming familiar with alpha (learning), gamma (discount), and epsilon (exploration) rates
- Diving into a classic RL problem, the **multi-armed bandit problem** (**MABP**), and putting it into a Q-learning context

Technical requirements

You will need the following packages installed to complete the exercises in this chapter. We will not be writing code as part of the exercises for this chapter, but we will provide some short coding examples from later chapters that will be useful for you to familiarize yourself with:

- Python 3.5+
- NumPy
- OpenAI Gym (please refer to Chapter 3, *Setting Up Your First Environment with OpenAI Gym,* for installation and setup instructions)

 We strongly encourage you to familiarize yourself with the official OpenAI Gym documentation for the Taxi-v2 environment and the other environments that we will be working with in this book. You will find a great deal of useful information on these environments and how to access the information and functionality you need from them. You can find the documentation at https://gym.openai.com/docs/.

The code for the exercises in this book can be found at https://github.com/ PacktPublishing/Hands-On-Q-Learning-with-Python/.

We will start developing our code in Chapter 3, *Setting Up Your First Environment with OpenAI Gym,* but some code snippets will be included in this chapter for illustration purposes. You will find all the code in this chapter in the Chapter 3, *Setting Up Your First Environment with OpenAI Gym,* section of the GitHub repository (https://github.com/ PacktPublishing/Hands-On-Q-Learning-with-Python/tree/master/Chapter03).

Demystifying MDPs

The technical purpose of Q-learning is to discover solutions for a type of optimization problem called an MDP.

When we talk about states and the actions that we can take from states, we are discussing concepts developed in the context of MDPs (and the Markov chains and other state space models that they are derived from).

Control processes

An MDP is itself a type of problem called a **control process**. Broadly speaking, a control process is designed to optimize a value or a set of values within a set of limitations. The following diagram shows a model for a generalized control process:

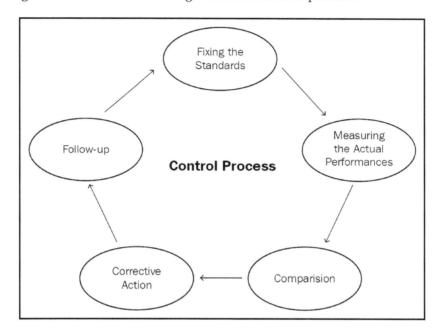

A real-world example of such an optimization process might be maximizing a company's profit by knowing its gross sales and variable expenses. We might want to keep expenses as low as possible without affecting the sales, and keep the sales as high as possible on a scale that we can manage without incurring too many new expenses.

An MDP models a set of states, a set of actions that can be taken from each state, and the outcome of taking each action. As the agent making the decisions in an MDP, part of the outcome of each action that we take is under our control, and part of it is random and unknown to us.

We will not go too deeply into the mathematical details of MDPs, but this information is worth digging into if you want a better understanding of how stochastic processes can be modeled in the context of Bayesian statistics, such as in Monte Carlo problems.

We will link to some useful resources on the mathematics of MDPs at the end of the chapter. For now, it will be sufficient to get an intuitive and visual understanding of them.

Markov chains

MDPs are based on Markov chains. A Markov chain is a model of a system of events where the probability of the next event depends only on the state of the previous event (or the current event).

Here's a very simple example of a process that can be modeled as a Markov chain. Suppose that we're playing a game with a binary outcome repeatedly—at the end of every round of the game, we will either win or lose:

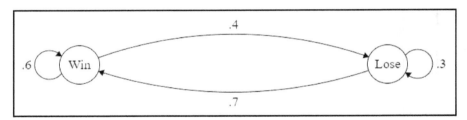

The chain has two states and the system moves back and forth between them. The arrows between them are the probabilities that we will move to the corresponding states. If we are in the **Win** state, there is a 60% chance that we will stay in **Win** and a 40% chance that we will move to **Lose** at the next timestep (the time it takes to play another round). Likewise, if we lose this round, there is a 70% chance that we will win the next round and a 30% chance that we will lose again.

As another example, suppose that we're playing a simple stochastic game that pays out rewards. Here is a partial state diagram of that game; we start in the state marked **$5**:

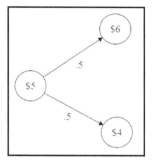

Every time we flip a fair coin, we win $1 if the coin comes up as heads or lose $1 if it comes up as tails. We start with $5 and flip the coin three times. A more general version of this process is called a **random walk**. The following tree diagram demonstrates a two-step random walk with a coin flip:

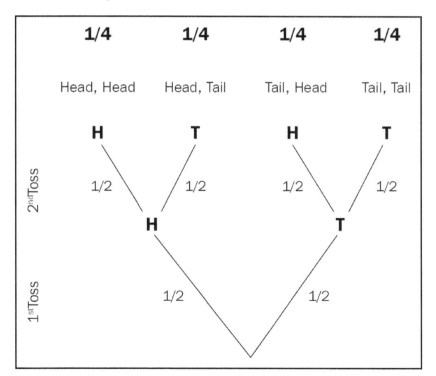

The following are the results when we flip the coin three times:

- First flip: Heads – $1 win
- Second flip: Tails – $1 loss
- Third flip: Heads – $1 win

We now have $6; we can think of this as our current state, which we will call S_0. From this state, we can go to one of two states, as follows:

- S_1: The state of having $5 – 50% probability
- S_2: The state of having $7 – 50% probability

The event that will cause us to go into one of these two states is a coin flip; that is, it is a stochastic event that has a probability of 50% for either outcome (because we have defined this as a fair coin).

We know the current state we are in (the state of having $6) and the two possible outcomes that will result from the coin flip event (either having $5 or having $7). Note that although we have continuously been playing this game and our current state depends on the previous states that we have been in, we don't need to know how much money we started with (or how much we won or lost previously) to know how much we will have on the next flip and what the probability is of either outcome.

In other words, we do not need knowledge of previous states to determine what the next state will be. Whatever our knowledge of previous states, our probability calculation for the next state will always be the same.

This memorylessness is the defining characteristic of a problem that can be modeled as a Markov chain. If I have $X now, I know for sure that I will have either $X+1 or $X-1 after the next coin flip. It doesn't matter if I had $X+1 or $X-1 after the previous coin flip; for the purposes of predicting what I will get next, all that matters is what I have now. Knowing about the past will not change my predictions about the future.

The Markov property

A Markov chain has the following characteristic, called the Markov property:

$$P[S_{t+1}|S_t] = P[S_{t+1}|S_1,\ldots,S_t]$$

This states, mathematically, that the likelihood distribution of the next state depends only on the current state and not on previous states. Given our knowledge of the current state, S_t, the probability of reaching S_{t+1} is the same as the probability of reaching $St+1$, given the knowledge of all the previous states.

To illustrate this further, let's talk about a different stochastic system where the Markov property won't apply. For example, we are working on a job site and have three pieces of equipment that we might be assigned at random over the course of three days. The equipment is given to us without a replacement in the original pool of equipment being assigned. There are two pieces of functioning equipment and one piece that is non-functioning:

Day 1	Functioning	Functioning	Non-functioning
Day 2	Non-functioning	Functioning	Functioning
Day 3	Functioning	Non-functioning	Functioning

If we're assigned non-functioning equipment on **Day 1**, we know for sure that on **Day 2** we will be assigned functioning equipment, since we know there are only three potential pieces that we could have been assigned.

On the other hand, if we come onto the job site starting on **Day 2** and are assigned functioning equipment, with no knowledge of what happened on **Day 1**, we know that we have a 50% probability of getting either functioning or non-functioning equipment on **Day 3**. If we did have knowledge of what happened on **Day 1** (that is, if we received either functioning or non-functioning equipment) we would know for sure what we would receive on **Day 3**.

Because our knowledge of the probability of each outcome changes with the knowledge that we have of this system, it does not have the Markov property. Knowing information about the past changes our prediction of the future.

You can think of a system having the Markov property as memoryless. Having more information about the past will not change our prediction of the future. If we change the system that we just described to make sure that the equipment that is given to us is replaced, the system will have the Markov property. There are now many outcomes that are available to us that weren't before:

Day 1	Functioning	Non-functioning	Functioning	Non-functioning
Day 2	Functioning	Functioning	Non-functioning	Non-functioning
Day 3	Functioning	Non-functioning	Non-functioning	Functioning

In this case, if the only information we have is that we were assigned functioning equipment on **Day 2**, then on **Day 3**, we know we have a 50% chance of getting functioning equipment or non-functioning equipment.

Note that this probability calculation does not depend on the specific examples that we've chosen for the preceding chart! Think about flipping a fair coin 100 times; even if you get heads every single time, your odds of getting tails the next time are still 50%, if you're really dealing with a fair coin. Similarly, even if we are assigned non-functioning equipment every single day, our probability of getting functioning equipment the next day will still be 50%.

We can neatly model our new system as follows:

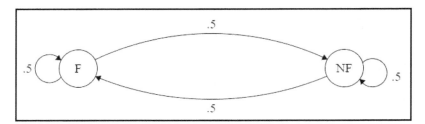

If we are in state **F** today, we have a 50% chance of staying in state **F** or moving to state **NF**, and vice versa. Notice that this is true no matter how much information we include in our probability calculation. Previous events do not affect the probability of future events.

MDPs and state-action diagrams

Note that in the Markov chain examples we discussed, there is only one event that can happen in each state to cause the system to move to the next state. There is no list of actions and no decisions to make about what action to take. In a random walk, we flip the same fair coin each time, and each time we flip the coin, we have a new pair of states that we can potentially enter.

An MDP adds to a Markov chain the presence of a decision-making agent that has a choice of what action to take and rewards to receive, and provides feedback to the agent, affecting its behavior. Recall that an MDP doesn't require any knowledge of any previous states to make a decision on what action to take from the current state.

Let's go back to the state diagram that we discussed in the last chapter. Notice that a state diagram for an MDP is necessarily more complex than a diagram for a Markov chain. It needs to represent the available action and rewards, and the different states that the system can be in:

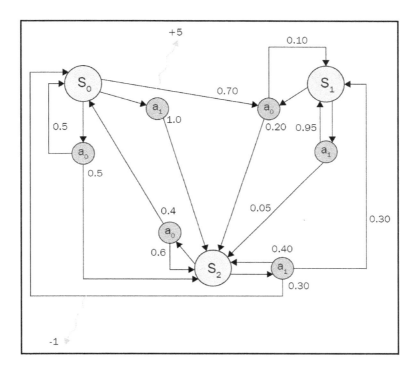

As we discussed, we have three states and two actions in this environment. Either action can be taken from any state, and the probability of each outcome as a result of taking each action is labeled on the diagram. For example, when we are in state S_0 and take action a_0, we might end up in S_2 or back in S_0, each with a 50% probability.

By extension, an MDP that only allows one action from each state and has the same reward for each action (that is, effectively, no rewards at all) will simplify to a Markov chain.

The main takeaway from this discussion of MDPs is that when we assume the role of an agent navigating a stochastic environment, we need to be able to learn lessons and make decisions that can be applied consistently amid the occurrence of random events. We don't always know what the individual outcome of an action will be, but we need to be able to make decisions that will maximize our overall outcome at each step of the process. This is what the algorithms that we develop will work toward achieving.

Solving MDPs with RL

RL algorithms are designed to solve exactly the type of optimization problem an MDP frames; that is, to find an optimal decision-making policy to maximize the rewards offered by making decisions within this environment.

The rewards offered for taking each action are shown in the preceding MDP diagram as yellow arrows. When we take action a_0 and end up in state S_0, we get a reward of **+5**; and when we take action a_1 and end up in state S_0, we get a reward of **-1**.

The Taxi-v2 environment has 500 states, as we'll see shortly, so it is not practical to represent them all in a diagram such as the previous one. Instead, we will be enumerating them in our Q-table in the next section. We'll use a state vector to represent the variables in each state that we'll be keeping track of.

In general, we can keep track of any variables in a Q-learning problem that we think are relevant for our model, and incorporate them into the state vector. The state vector can be treated as a set of state variables, and it can also be treated as a set of linear numbered states, as long as the individual information about each state is not lost, no matter how the vector information is stored:

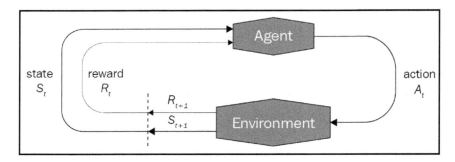

The preceding diagram models how agents and environments act with each other in a general way; an agent is in a state, takes an action on its environment, and then receives a reward and moves to a new state. In control process terms, the environment acts on the agent through state and reward information, and the agent acts on the state through actions.

In the case of Taxi-v2 and other OpenAI Gym environments that we'll be using, the state space is predetermined for us, so we do not have to decide what state variables to keep track of or how to enumerate our states. In an environment that we have designed on our own, we will have to choose how to model these attributes ourselves as efficiently as possible.

We will also see that in the problems we are working with, we don't need knowledge of any previous states to determine what actions to take in our current state. Every state can be represented by a state variable, and every action is available in an action space that the agent can choose and act on with only the knowledge of the current state.

Your Q-learning agent in its environment

Let's talk about the self-driving taxi agent that we'll be building. Recall that the Taxi-v2 environment has 500 states, and 6 possible actions that can be taken from each state.

Your objective in the taxi environment is to pick up a passenger at one location, and drop them off at their desired destination in as few timesteps as possible.

You receive points for a successful drop-off, and lose points for the time it takes to complete the task, so your goal is to complete the task in as little time as possible. You also lose points for incorrect actions, such as dropping a passenger off at the wrong location.

Because your goal is to get to both the pickup and drop-off locations as quickly as possible, you lose one point for every move you make per timestep.

Your agent's goal in solving this problem is to find the optimal policy for getting the passenger to their destination as efficiently as possible, netting the maximum reward for itself. While it navigates the environment, it will learn the best action to take from each state, which will serve as its policy function.

Remember that because Q-learning is value-based and not policy-based, it will not take your agent's actual policy into account, and we will not explicitly enumerate this policy. Instead, the Q-learning algorithm will calculate the value for each state-action pair based on the highest possible value of the next action that your agent could take, therefore assuming that your agent is already following the optimal policy.

We will continue to explore this concept in more detail with the functions that you will write for your agent. The OpenAI Gym package that we will use will provide the game environment, and you will implement the Q-learning algorithm yourself. You can then use the same environment to implement other RL algorithms and compare their performance.

Solving the optimization problem

Every time your agent steps through the environment, it will update the Q-table with the rewards it has received. Once your Q-table stops updating and reaches its final state, we will know that your agent has found the optimal path to its destination. It will have solved the MDP represented by its environment.

What this means in practice is that your agent will have found the best actions to take from each state that it has encountered through its exploration of its environment. It will have learned enough about the environment to have found an optimal strategy for navigating a path to the goal. When your Q-table stops updating, we say that it has converged to its final state.

We can be sure that when the Q-table converges, then the agent has found the optimal solution. Q-learning, as we've discussed, is only one learning algorithm that can find a solution to the problem, and there are others that are sometimes more efficient or faster. The reason that we choose to use Q-learning as our introduction to RL is that it is relatively simple, straightforward to learn, and it gives us a good introduction to the types of problems that we'll be facing in this optimization space.

States and actions in Taxi-v2

So, what are the 500 states that the taxi environment can be in, and what are the actions it can take from those states? Let's take a look at this in action.

You instantiate a taxi environment in OpenAI Gym. In the following screenshot, the small grid underneath the code block is your game environment. The yellow rectangle represents the taxi agent, and the four letters indicate the pickup and drop-off locations for your passengers:

```
import gym
env = gym.make "Taxi-v2"
env.render()

+---------+
|R: | : :G|
| : : : : |
| : : : : |
| | : | : |
|Y| : |B: |
+---------+
```

We have a 5 x 5 game grid, which entails the following:

- There are 25 possible spaces for the taxi agent to be in at any time.
- There are 5 locations for the passenger to be in (such as inside the taxi or at any of the 4 drop-off points).
- There are 4 possible correct destinations (as opposed to locations that the passenger does not want to be dropped off at).

This gives *25 x 5 x 4 = 500* possible states.

The state we are enumerating could, therefore, be represented with the following state vector:

   S = <taxi location, passenger location, destination location>

The three variables in the state vector represent the three factors that could change in each state.

Some of the states that we'll enumerate in our list of 500 are unreachable. For example, if the passenger is at the correct destination, then that iteration of the game is over. The taxi must also be at the destination at that point, since this is a Terminal state and the taxi will not make any additional moves. So, any state that has the passenger at the destination and the taxi at a different location will never be encountered, but we still represent these states in the state space for simplicity.

The six possible actions in Taxi-v2 are as follows:

- South (0)
- North (1)
- East (2)
- West (3)
- Pickup (4)
- Drop-off (5)

These actions are discrete and deterministic; at each step, we choose an action to take based on the Q-learning algorithm we will design and implement. If we have no algorithm in place yet, we can choose to take a random action. Notice that we cannot take every possible action from every state. We cannot turn left (that is, west) if there is a wall to our left, for example.

We reset the environment and go to a random state when we start an episode:

```
state = env.reset()
```

The agent chooses an action to take in the environment, and every time it does, the environment returns four variables:

- `observation`: This refers to the new state that we are in.
- `reward`: This indicates the reward that we have received.
- `done`: This tells us whether we have successfully dropped off the passenger at the correct location.
- `info`: This provides us with any additional information that we may need for debugging.

We collect these variables as follows:

```
observation, reward, done, info = env.step(env.action_space.sample())
```

This will cause the agent to take one step through the task loop and have the environment return the required variables. It will be useful to keep track of these variables and report them as we step through our taxi model, which we'll start building in the next chapter.

A potential taxi reward structure might work as follows:

- A reward of +20 for successfully dropping off the passenger
- A penalty of 10 for an incorrect pickup or drop-off (that is, a reward of -10)
- A reward of -1 for all other actions, such as moving forward one step

The longer the agent takes to execute a successful drop-off, the more points it will lose. We don't want it to take unnecessary steps, but we also don't want it to make illegal moves by trying to reach the destination faster, so the penalty for taking a non-drop-off step is small. An optimal solution will be to have the agent reach the correct destination in the minimum number of timesteps.

Again, once the Q-table converges to its final values and stops updating with each iteration, the agent will have discovered the optimal path to reaching the destination as quickly as possible.

Fine-tuning your model – learning, discount, and exploration rates

Recall our discussion of the three major hyperparameters of a Q-learning model:

- **Alpha**: The learning rate
- **Gamma**: The discount rate
- **Epsilon**: The exploration rate

What values should we choose for these hyperparameters to optimize the performance of our taxi agent? We will discover these values through experimentation once we have constructed our game environment, and we can also take advantage of existing research on the taxi problem and set the variables to known optimal values.

A large part of our model-tuning and optimization phase will consist of comparing the performance of different combinations of these three hyperparamenters together.

One option that we have is the ability to decay any, or all, of these hyperparameters – in other words, to reduce their values as we progress through a game loop or conduct repeated trials. In practice, we will almost always decay epsilon, since we want our agent to adapt to the knowledge it has of its environment and explore less as it becomes better aware of the highest-valued actions to take. But it can sometimes be to our benefit to decay the other hyperparameters as well.

Decaying epsilon

We've discussed epsilon decay in the context of exploration versus exploitation. The more we get to know our environment, the less random exploration we want to do and the more actions we want to take that we know will give us high rewards. Our goal should always be to take advantage of what we already know.

We do this by reducing the agent's epsilon value by a particular amount as the game progresses. Remember that epsilon is the likelihood (in percentage) that the agent will take a random action, instead of taking the current highest Q-valued action for the current state.

When we reduce epsilon, the likelihood of a random action becomes smaller, and we take more opportunities to benefit from the high-valued actions that we have already discovered.

For similar reasons, it can be to our benefit to decay alpha and gamma along with epsilon.

Decaying alpha

In a totally deterministic environment, we will want to keep alpha at 1 at all times, since we already know that *alpha = 1* will cause the agent to learn the best policy for that environment. But, in a stochastic environment, including most of the environments that we will be working in when we build Q-learning models, decaying alpha based on what we have already learned can allow our algorithm to converge faster.

In practice, for a problem such as this, we are unlikely to decay alpha in the course of running an environment, as the noticeable benefits will be negligible. We will see this in action when we begin choosing values for the hyperparameters.

For the taxi problem, we are likely to start with an alpha such as 0.1 and progressively compare it to higher values. We could also run a programmatic method, such as a cross-validated grid search, to identify the optimal hyperparameter values that allow the algorithm to converge fastest.

Decaying gamma

Decaying gamma will have the agent prioritize short-term rewards as it learns what those rewards are, and puts less emphasis on long-term rewards.

Remember that a gamma value of 0 will cause an agent to totally disregard future values and focus only on current rewards, and that a gamma value of 1 will cause it to prioritize future values in the same way as current ones. Decaying gamma will, therefore, increase its focus onto current rewards and away from future rewards.

Intuitively, this benefits us, because the closer we get to our goal, the more we want to take advantage of these short-term rewards instead of holding out for future rewards that won't be available after we complete the task. We can reach our goal faster and more efficiently by changing the use of the resources that we have available to us as the availability of those resources changes.

MABP – a classic exploration versus exploitation problem

Several MABP environments have been created for OpenAI Gym, and they are well worth exploring for a clearer picture of how the problem works. We will not be solving a bandit problem from scratch with the code in this book, but we will go into some solutions in detail and discuss their relevance to epsilon decay strategies.

The main thing to bear in mind when solving any bandit problem is that we are always trying to discover the optimal outcome in a system by balancing our need to both explore and exploit our knowledge of our environment. Effectively, we are learning as we go and we are taking advantage of the knowledge that we already have in the process of gaining new knowledge.

Setting up a bandit problem

A straightforward MABP involves encountering a slot machine with n arms (alternatively, a row of n one-armed machines). We have a set amount of money to put in these machines and we want to maximize our payout. We keep track of which machines pay out each time and keep a probability distribution of each machine's payout.

When we start playing, we don't know which of these arms will pay out more than others; the only way we can find that out is by playing each one and observing long-term how often they pay out. What strategy should we use to decide which arms to pull, when to pull them, and when to prioritize one arm over others?

For simplicity, let's assume that each time you pull an arm, you get a reward of either $1 or $0 (a bandit with a payout of either **1** or **0** is called a *Bernoulli bandit*). With a particular 4-armed bandit, we might get the following results:

Arm	Reward
1	0
2	1
3	0
4	1
2	0
4	1
4	1
2	0
1	1

In the preceding simulation, we start out in exploration mode (meaning that we have a high epsilon value), so we try all four arms at once. We get no reward from arms **1** and **3**, but we do get rewards from **2** and **4**. We pull **2** again hoping for another reward, but we don't get one. We pull **4** again and get a reward, and now it looks like **4** is a good arm, so we pull it again and get another reward.

By the end of the trial, we have the following results:

- **Arm 1**: 2 pulls, 1 win, and 50% success
- **Arm 2**: 3 pulls, 1 win, and 33% success
- **Arm 3**: 1 pull, 0 wins, and 0% success
- **Arm 4**: 3 pulls, 3 wins, and 100% success

Based on these results, we now have some reason to believe **4** is a good arm to pull and that **2** is not necessarily very good. We have a 0% chance of a reward outcome from **3**; however, because we have only pulled it once, we should pull it more to get more information about it before making a decision.

Similarly, we have a 50% chance of a reward outcome from **1**, but since we have only pulled it twice, we probably don't have enough information yet to decide whether it is a good arm to pull. We will need to run the game for more rounds in order to be able to make useful predictions about the arms that we don't yet know enough about.

As we continue to play, we keep track of our results, and eventually, we build up a probability distribution of wins for each arm with enough observations so that we can rely on the results. This becomes the exploitation side of our strategy, and we want to make sure we play arms that we know are likely to win as often as possible, even while we continue to explore the results for other arms.

Bandit optimization strategies

One strategy for deciding which arm to pull at this point is a simple greedy strategy; that is, pull the arm that currently looks best and don't worry about any of the other arms. This is, of course, a naive approach, because although arm **4** might currently look like the best arm to pull, we don't know yet whether any of the other arms will be better than **4**.

An even worse outcome might be that since **2** was the first arm that we pulled that gave us a reward, we might decide to keep pulling it forever and never discover a potentially better arm such as **4**. In optimization problems, we call this getting stuck on a local maximum, as illustrated in the following diagram.

When we are stuck on a local maximum, all of the reward values we see near us are less than our current reward value, so from our limited information state we think that we have reached an optimal path and should stay there and continue to collect rewards. From where we are, we can't see the global maximum that could give us more rewards if we were to seek it out and locate it:

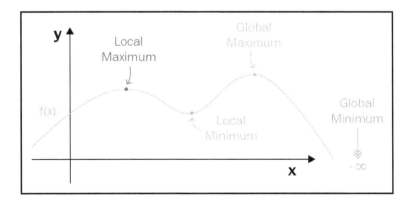

Getting stuck on a local maximum happens when an agent continually takes stock of its available actions and chooses the same one over and over because it happens to be the current highest value. Because it cannot reach any states from where it is, this will give it enough information to increase the value of the other actions – note that it can never discover any values higher than the current local maximum if it does not branch out and take other actions.

There are other, better, strategies than the greedy strategy that we will use, starting with the epsilon-greedy strategy, which we will discuss in depth at the beginning of the Chapter 7, *Decoupling Exploration and Exploitation in Multi-Armed Bandits*, on solving bandit problems. Let's cover it briefly here.

Remember that epsilon is the probability that we will take an action other than the current highest Q-valued action. Using the epsilon-greedy strategy, when epsilon = 0.1, an agent will choose the current highest Q-valued machine with the probability of 0.9 (1 - epsilon) and any other machine with the probability of 0.1.

We can set the epsilon to any value we choose, and we can choose to decay it over time as we conduct repeated trials. As we'll see in our example implementations, epsilon-greedy strategies suffer when the agent gets stuck exploring a suboptimal path before it gets a chance to explore all paths and find the best one. Our goal will be to find a strategy that efficiently gets us to an optimal explore-exploit balance and brings us as quickly as possible to the highest-yielding action gradients (that is exploitation paths).

Other applications for bandit problems

One of the most well-known applications of the MABP methodology is in recommendation systems. For example, an advertiser's goal using a process such as A/B testing is to compare several alternative online advertisements and choose the one that performs best among users.

In A/B testing, we split our audience into similar groups and test different versions of ads on each group to compare their performance. In an advertising scenario, one online ad is treated as a control and another is treated as a test, similar to common experimental design in scientific testing. The control should be an ad of which the performance is known and can be measured against some established standard, and the test ads are then compared against the control ad.

As an alternative to A/B testing, we could set up the question of which ads users will click on as an MABP, where each ad is a potential source of revenue and the goal is to decide when and how often to deploy each ad to maximize total revenue. In this process, we are benefiting from our knowledge of target user behavior at the same time that we are observing and learning about that behavior.

Optimal versus safe paths – revisiting SARSA

We discussed optimal goal-seeking strategies in the context of the MABP, but let's now discuss them more generally:

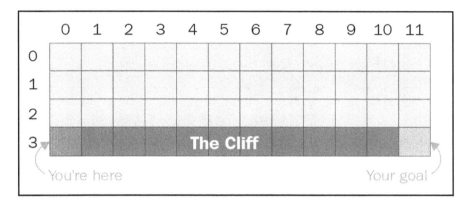

As we briefly discussed in Chapter 1, *Brushing Up on Reinforcement Learning Concepts*, regarding the differences between Q-learning and **State-Action-Reward-State-Action** (**SARSA**), we can sum those differences up as follows: Q-learning takes the optimal path to the goal, while SARSA takes a suboptimal but safer path, with less risk of taking highly suboptimal actions.

In the well-known cliff-walking problem, the goal is to start at the bottom left square in the preceding diagram and get to the bottom right square while getting the highest score possible. If you step on a blue square, then you get a penalty of -100 points, and if you step on a gray square, then you get a penalty of -1 points.

Here, the optimal path is to move one square up from the green square to the gray square (2, 0), move 11 squares to the left to (2, 11), and finally, move one square down to the orange square (3, 11). We are effectively running right along the edge of the cliff—just one step away from falling off.

Q-learning is designed to find and take this optimal path. In discovering this path, it will likely use some exploration algorithm such as epsilon-greedy, giving in a nonzero probability of taking a random action at any step.

This means that while the agent is in row **2**, there is a nonzero chance that it will take a random action and simply step off the cliff, causing a large penalty. Ideally, we want some way to guard against suboptimal actions with such huge penalties.

One solution is to use SARSA instead. Instead of assuming that the agent will take the maximum-valued action from the next state, as Q-learning does, SARSA finds the actual action the agent takes from the next state and incorporates that value into the Q-value of the current state.

Here's a pseudocode version of how Q-learning updates the Q-table:

```
define update Q-table (current_state, action, reward, next_state):
    maxQ = maximum Q-value for all actions from next_state
    current Q value for current_state = reward + discount factor * maxQ
```

We'll go through the specifics of this in Chapter 4, *Teaching a Smartcab to Drive Using Q-Learning*. For now, it's only important to notice the difference between the preceding pseudocode snippet and the SARSA version:

```
define update Q-table (current_state, action, reward, next_state,
next_action):
    nextQ = Q-value for next_action from next_state
    current Q value for current_state = reward + discount factor * nextQ
```

The only change we've made is adding in a next_action parameter and using the Q-value of that next action in place of the action with the highest Q-value. This means that, unlike Q-learning, SARSA does not assume the agent will take the highest-valued next action, but finds out what action the agent actually takes, and updates the Q-value for the current state-action pair based on that.

This is a subtle difference, but it leads to a huge difference in performance when there is a high chance that an agent might take suboptimal actions with large penalties. Being able to guard against those penalties allows it to follow a safer policy that protects it from an unacceptably high level of risk.

Summary

Q-learning is an algorithm designed to solve an MDP; that is, a type of control problem that seeks to optimize a variable within a set of constraints. An MDP is built on a Markov chain; a state model in which determining the probability distribution of reaching future states does not require knowledge of any previous states beyond the current one.

An MDP builds on a Markov chain by introducing actions and rewards that can be taken by a learning agent, and allows for choice and decision-making in a stochastic process. Q-learning, as well as other RL algorithms, models the state space of an MDP and progressively reaches an optimal solution by simulating the decisions of a learning agent working within the constraints of the model.

In the next chapter, we'll explore the OpenAI Gym package, the different environments we'll be using, and get comfortable working with the functions that are available to us. We'll set up everything we need to get started on our first Q-learning project in `Chapter 4`, *Teaching a Smartcab to Drive Using Q-Learning*.

Questions

1. Define a control process.
2. What is the difference between a Markov chain and an MDP?
3. What does it mean for a system to have the Markov property? Explain this in the context of memorylessness.
4. Explain why the Taxi-v2 environment has 500 states. Describe the three state variables and enumerate the state space.
5. Why are some states unreachable and why do we include them in our description of the state space?
6. Describe a systematic way to choose the optimal hyperparameters for a Q-learning model.
7. Why do we choose to decay epsilon, and how do we refer to the decision-making phenomenon that results?
8. What type of environment will an alpha value of 1 be ideal for? What will an alpha value of 0 result in?
9. What is one good reason to decay gamma? Why might you want a lower value for gamma toward the end of a simulation?

10. Briefly describe the greedy strategy and give an example of an agent enacting it within a single timestep.

11. Under what circumstances does the epsilon-greedy strategy perform poorly?

12. What does it mean to get stuck on a local maximum, and what is one way to avoid doing this?

13. What is A/B testing?

3
Setting Up Your First Environment with OpenAI Gym

For your first project, you will be designing a Q-learning agent to navigate an environment from the OpenAI Gym package in Python. Gym provides the environment with all the available states and actions, while you provide the Q-learning algorithm that solves the task presented by the environment.

Using Gym will allow you to build **reinforcement learning** (**RL**) models, compare their performance in a standardized setting, and keep track of updated versions. It will also allow others to track your work and performance, and compare it to their own.

In this chapter, we will show you how to set up your Gym programming environment and what you will need to get started. We will also implement a randomly-acting agent to serve as our baseline model and to compare with our learning models.

We will cover the following topics in this chapter:

- Learning how to install OpenAI Gym in your Python 3.5+ environment
- Getting started by setting up a Taxi-v2 instance
- Becoming familiar with the functionality of Gym and implementing a game loop that allows an agent to take random actions to compare its performance to that of a Q-learning agent

Technical requirements

You will need the following installed to complete the exercises in this chapter:

- Python 3.5+
- OpenAI Gym

The code for the exercises in this chapter can be found at https://github.com/ PacktPublishing/Hands-On-Q-Learning-with-Python/tree/master/Chapter03.

Getting started with OpenAI Gym

In this section, we'll get familiar with the OpenAI Gym package and learn how to get it up and running in your Python development environment.

What is Gym?

OpenAI Gym is a toolkit of **environments** for building RL algorithms. In the context of RL, an environment refers to the actual task (a **Markov decision process** or **MDP**) that is to be solved by the algorithm. The state and action spaces of the task are defined by the environment.

Be careful not to get the RL use of the word *environment* confused with others that we might use in different contexts, such as a Python development environment or a Unix/Linux environment. Those terms refer to very different things.

The following diagram shows the basic structure of a Gym environment:

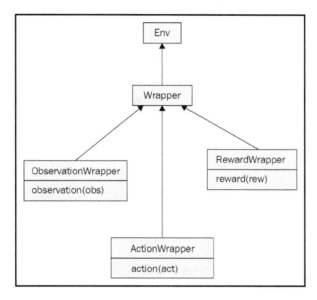

The agent that you build will take **actions** against the environment, and the environment will return **observations** (also called **states**) and **rewards**. The process is shown as follows:

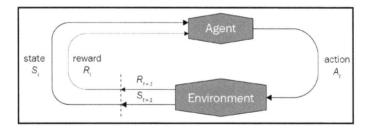

Setting up Gym

You have two options for setting up OpenAI Gym to use with your Python programming environment: installing from `pip`, or cloning the source and installing the full repository.

Cloning the source is recommended if you want to modify a Gym environment or add environments yourself. When you first start using Gym, we recommend that you install using `pip` to get started and familiarize yourself with the package as quickly as possible.

You can install Gym using `pip` in a Terminal as follows; you'll need to make sure that you have Python 3.5+ already installed:

```
pip install gym
```

At this point, you are done, and can skip directly to the *Setting up an environment* part of this section.

To clone the source directly from GitHub, use the following command:

```
git clone https://github.com/openai/gym
cd gym
pip install -e .
```

You can then do a full installation using the method that you prefer from the official Gym documentation at https://github.com/openai/gym#installing-everything.

 All of the code from this chapter can be found in the GitHub repository that is linked in the *Technical requirements* section of this chapter.

Gym environments

OpenAI Gym tasks are available as environments that provide us with a state space and an action space, along with the rewards and outcome responses that we need to train a learning agent.

There are many environments to work with; some that are simpler to use and understand than others, and new environments are being added continually. We discussed many of these different environments in detail in the last chapter:

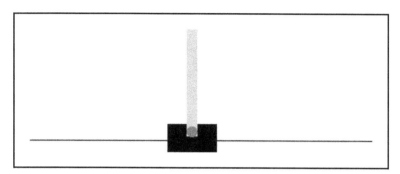

The preceding diagram is a still from the CartPole environment, a task that we'll be solving in Chapter 6, *Digging Deeper into Deep Q-Networks with Keras and TensorFlow,* using a deep Q-network.

The CartPole task is simple: a pole is balanced on a cart and can rotate freely. The goal is to move the cart back and forth to keep the pole upright (that is, no more than 15 degrees from the vertical). As we'll see in Chapter 6, *Digging Deeper into Deep Q-Networks with Keras and TensorFlow,* representing the state space of this environment will quickly become complex, as it has an infinite number of states.

An environment, at a minimum, consists of a set of states, and actions that can be taken from each of those states. The simplest toy text environments in Gym contain as few as 16 states, and the most complex continuous control environments consist of effectively an infinite number of states.

Setting up an environment

For our first Q-learning implementation, we'll be solving the Taxi-v2 task. Let's go through how to get this project set up.

In the Taxi-v2 environment, your agent is a self-driving taxicab whose job it is to collect passengers from their locations and drop them off at their chosen destinations:

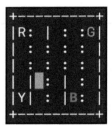

To perform this task optimally, the taxi must do the following:

- Find the passenger in the shortest time possible and pick the passenger up.
- Drive the passenger to their destination in the shortest time possible and drop the passenger off.

The taxi receives a reward of 20 points for reaching the correct destination and dropping off the passenger. It loses 10 points for an incorrect pickup or dropoff, and it loses 1 point for all other actions, including moving one space in any direction. The penalty for a non-dropoff action provides an incentive for the taxi to complete the task in as few timesteps as possible.

To get started exploring the `Taxi-v2` environment, import the `gym` package, load the environment, and then initialize it.

We're using a Jupyter Notebook for these examples, and all of our screenshots are taken directly from the notebook. If you prefer not to use a notebook, you can use a Python interpreter or create a `.py` script to run these commands:

```
import gym
env = gym.make('Taxi-v2')
state = env.reset()
```

`env` is your environment object and contains the built-in information that you will need about your state-action space and the functions you can call within it. The `gym.make()` function creates your environment and returns this object.

`env.reset()` resets the environment's state and returns a variable that we will call `state`. Recall that the state we are in (also called an observation) is one of the environment variables that we will be getting back for each action we take. The state or observation variable will be a number between 0 and 499 that corresponds to the state we are now in, which will be a random state each time the function is called.

The following line lets us see the value of `state`; it will be a different random value between 0 and 499 every time we run `env.reset()`:

```
print(state)
```

We render the environment onscreen, as follows:

```
env.render()
```

You will see the following representation of the game environment:

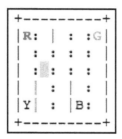

The yellow rectangle represents the taxi in its current location; when the taxi has a passenger, it will show as green. The four letters represent destinations that can be either pickup or drop-off locations.

Therefore, each state variable tells us three things:

- Where the taxi is now (out of 25 possibilities)
- Where the passenger is now (inside the taxi or at one of the four locations marked R, G, B, or Y)
- Where the passenger's destination is (R, G, B, or Y)

This gives us *25 x 5 x 4 = 500 distinct states*.

So, what happens when we run `env.reset()` again? Take a look at the following screenshot:

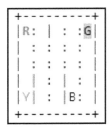

We see that the taxi agent has moved to a different random location. In the same way as when we called it before, `env.reset()` will put us in a random state and return the value for the state we are now in, which is a number between 0 and 499.

Exploring the Taxi-v2 environment

In this section, we'll be going through how a Gym environment works, and some of the functions and environment variables that you'll be making use of.

Note that we will sometimes use the words state and observation interchangeably. We use **state** as the conventional term referring to the current condition of a finite-state machine, including the MDPs that we are representing and solving with Q-learning, and we use **observation** when it is the term that is used in the Gym package itself, as in the following example:

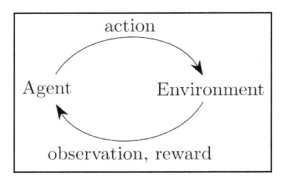

Both state and observation in this context refer to the same thing.

The state space and valid actions

We get the number of states and actions from the environment with the following two variables:

```
env.observation_space
env.action_space
```

As mentioned previously, we will usually use the term **state** to follow convention, but the environment variable will be called an **observation**. These terms can be treated as interchangeable in this context, as shown in the following screenshot:

```
print("Action Space {}".format(env.action_space))
print("State Space {}".format(env.observation_space))

Action Space Discrete(6)
State Space Discrete(500)
```

Both the `Action Space` and the `State Space` attributes referenced in the preceding screenshot are of type `gym.spaces.discrete.Discrete`. You can find out more information about these attribute types from the official Gym documentation.

We strongly recommend that you familiarize yourself with the Gym documentation as you work through the projects in this book and on further projects of your own.

Recall the six valid action values, as follows:

- 0: South
- 1: North
- 2: East
- 3: West
- 4: Pickup
- 5: Drop-off

In the next section, we will step through the environment with `env.step()`, which takes an action value as an argument. We'll generate a valid action from the action space using `env.action_space.sample()`, which randomly selects an action from the space and returns it as an integer value.

Choosing an action manually

We will run these following two lines in a notebook:

```
env.step(1)
env.render()
```

The following is the result for the preceding code:

```
env.step(1)

(382, -1, False, {'prob': 1.0})


env.render

+---------+
|R: | : :G|
| : : : : |
| : : : : |
| | : | :▒|
|Y| : |B: |
+---------+
   (North)
```

`env.step(1)` returns the following four variables:

- `observation`: This refers to the new state that we are in (that is, state `382`).
- `reward`: This refers to the reward that we have received (`-1`).
- `done`: This tells us whether we have successfully dropped off the passenger at the correct location (`False`).
- `info`: This provides any additional information that we may need for debugging.

Note that we chose an argument of 1 for `env.step()` specifically, because we wanted the agent to move `north`. Choosing a different value for this function will send the agent in a different direction.

In practice, we will not be manually setting action values; instead, we will let the algorithm that we are running choose them for us, whether they are random actions or actions with high Q-values.

Setting a state manually

We can manually set the state of the environment by changing the state variable. Note that you should not set the state manually when running this task; this is bad practice and is not encouraged by OpenAI Gym. We are demonstrating it here for illustration purposes only:

```
env.env.s = 20
env.render()
```

The following is the result for the preceding code:

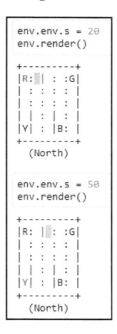

Generally, in a game loop, we will be sent to the state that results from taking an action selected by the Q-learning algorithm and will not need to set the state manually. In this demonstration, it can be useful to verify for yourself that each value corresponds to a fixed state in the task.

You can set the states to the values that we have used to confirm that the result is the same as what we have here. We see that in state 20, the taxi is one space to the right of the location marked R, and in state 50, it is two spaces to the right of location R.

In the preceding diagram, we aren't shown the location of the passenger or which of the four marked locations is designated the destination, but those variables are stored as part of the state information. Each of the 500 states will have a unique set of values for these variables.

Creating a baseline agent

In this section, we'll implement an agent that takes random actions and does not keep track of its actions or learn from them. We'll get started on building an actual Q-learning algorithm in Chapter 4, *Teaching a Smartcab to Drive Using Q-Learning*. For now, all your agent will be able to do is to take random actions.

As part of our analysis, we'll be comparing the success of this randomly-acting agent to the results of an optimized Q-learning agent. The randomly-acting agent is called our baseline agent, and we will use it as a control to which we'll compare the performance of future machine learning models. We'll discuss the significance of baseline models at the end of the chapter.

Stepping through actions

We can take a random action using env.action_space.sample(), as follows:

```
observation, reward, done, info = env.step(env.action_space.sample())
```

The env.action_space.sample() function returns a random action from the allowed actions. The env.step() function carries out this action and sends us to the next state.

Recall the four variables that we have collected from env.step():

- observation: This refers to the new state that we are in.
- reward: This indicates the reward that we have received.
- done: This tells us whether we have successfully dropped off the passenger at the correct location or whether we have taken the maximum number of steps.
- info: This provides additional information that we may need for debugging.

Let's take a look at these last few exercises in action; put your environment in state 50, as follows:

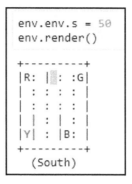

Then, take the 0 action step (that is, move south):

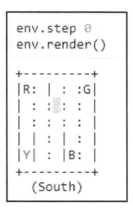

We see that the action step has caused the agent to move one space down; the env.step(0) function returns the following:

```
(150, -1, False, {'prob': 1.0})
```

We can store this as needed when we call the function.

According to our original call to `env.step()`, the variables are assigned as follows:

- `observation:` `150`
- `reward:` `-1`
- `done:` `False`
- `info:` `{'prob': 1.0}`

Looking at what the `env.step()` function has returned, we can see that we are now in state `150`, that we have gotten a reward of `-1`, and that we have not reached the destination yet.

The last value we see is the `info` variable, which we will not be making use of in this part of the project. In this case, it contains the probabilities behind the environment's last state change. You can get more information about this variable from the official Gym documentation.

Creating a task loop

In this section, we'll create our first task loop. We'll let our agent run by making random moves until it successfully reaches the goal of dropping off a passenger at the correct location.

Here is a simple way to implement a randomly-acting agent:

```
state = env.reset()
reward = 0
while reward != 20:
    observation, reward, done, info = env.step(env.action_space.sample())
env.render()
```

We reset the environment to put it into a random state for the start of the loop. We set the reward to zero, meaning that the goal has not yet been reached. We call `env.step()` repeatedly, with `env.action_space.sample()` as an argument to get a random action from the six allowable actions, and then advance the agent by one step. Finally, we set the ending condition for the loop at the point when the taxi receives a reward of `20`, meaning that it has dropped off the passenger at the correct location.

We get the following result when we render the environment after the game loop has exited:

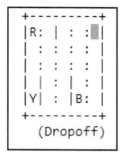

The taxi has just taken the **Dropoff** action at the **G** location, meaning that it has received a reward of 20 points and the game has ended, so the exit condition for the game loop has been met. Note that the taxi appears green instead of yellow on the screen, indicating that is currently carrying a passenger.

At this point, we know that the agent has taken a series of random actions and has eventually reached the goal. But what actions did it actually take, and how many steps did it take to get to the destination? These questions will be important when we compare it to our Q-learning agent and observe how each performs.

First, let's add a counter to this loop to see how many actions it took for the agent to reach the goal state:

```
observation = env.reset()
count = 0
reward = 0
while reward != 20:
    observation, reward, done, info = env.step(env.action_space.sample())
    count += 1
env.render()
```

The count variable now tells us how many steps the agent had to take to reach the goal:

```
print(count)
```

The following is the result for the preceding code:

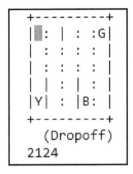

We see that in this run-through of the task loop, the agent took 2124 random actions to reach the destination!

At this point, the agent is not keeping track of any of its past actions and can't learn anything from them, so it is stuck starting from scratch every single time it makes a decision. We definitely want to improve on this.

If you want to know each action that the agent takes during the loop, one way to access each individual action is by calling env.render() at the end of the while loop, as follows:

```
observation = env.reset()
count = 0
reward = 0
while reward != 20:
    observation, reward, done, info = env.step(env.action_space.sample())
    count += 1
    env.render() #render each step of the game loop
```

This will render the game environment at each step, based on how many steps it takes for the agent to reach the destination. If you have a loop that takes thousands of iterations to complete, be aware that the environment will be rendered each time the loop runs, and make sure this is the behavior you intend.

For debugging purposes, if you only want the value of the action at each step, instead of calling env.render(), you can access the action from the return value of env.action_space.sample():

```
observation = env.reset()
count = 0
reward = 0
while reward != 20:
    action = env.action_space.sample()
```

```
observation, reward, done, info = env.step(action)
count += 1
print(action)
```

This will print the value of the action (between 0 and 5).

If you want to print the list of actions as strings for your own convenience, you can associate each number in env.action_space with the correct action using a map or dictionary; here is an example of how to do this:

```
taxi_actions = {
  0 : 'South',
  1 : 'North',
  2 : 'East',
  3 : 'West',
  4 : 'Pickup',
  5 : 'Dropoff'
}
```

For example, you could get the string value of a randomly-sampled action from the dictionary, as demonstrated in the following code. This can be useful if you want to record or print actions for debugging purposes during the task:

```
taxi_actions.get(env.action_space.sample())
```

Baseline models in Q-learning and machine learning research

In machine learning terminology, we refer to the randomly-acting agent that we have created in this chapter as a baseline model. A baseline is intended to give us a comparison metric to improve against. We use baseline models in machine learning to validate the performance of our current models against our past models.

Using a baseline model is good practice in scientific research, because we want to build on the progress that others have made, along with our own progress. As researchers, we start with the best available models of a scientific phenomenon and show how we can improve on their predictive capability. In this way, we create value for the scientific community by building on the continuity of existing research and putting our own work in the context of an existing knowledge base.

For our current model, we want a way to improve the baseline agent's performance by letting it keep track of what it did in the past, and what the results were, to inform its future decisions. This is where learning comes in.

In the next chapter, we will augment the randomly-acting agent with a Q-learning algorithm that causes it to calculate the highest Q-valued action for each state it is in, and modify the Q-table each time it takes a step.

Summary

We've set up the OpenAI Gym environment and have started exploring the basic functionality of the package. We've become familiar with the environment and now know how to put in place a learning agent that can take random actions in the environment that may or may not find an optimal solution to the problem, or may take an unreasonably long time to find it.

In the next chapter, we'll see how to implement Q-learning for this agent to make it reach a solution faster and more efficiently, and observe the effect on a Q-learning agent's performance the longer it runs and collects data over time.

Questions

1. How can you modify an environment or add additional environments to the Gym package?
2. Why have we chosen to use the terms state and observation interchangeably in this context?
3. What does `env.reset()` do and what does it return?
4. Under what conditions does the game loop that we created exit?
5. What variable do we set to manually change the state of the environment?
6. Why does a randomly-acting agent usually take longer than a learning agent to reach a destination?

4
Teaching a Smartcab to Drive Using Q-Learning

In this chapter, you will build and test your first Q-learning agent, a smartcab, using the Taxi-v2 environment from the OpenAI Gym package in Python.

Your agent is a self-driving taxicab whose job it is to collect passengers from a starting location and drop them off at their desired destination in the fewest steps possible. The taxi collects a reward when it drops off a passenger and gets penalties for taking other actions.

Gym provides the environment with all available states and actions and the attributes and functions you will need to use, and you provide the Q-learning algorithm that finds the optimal solution to the task.

Using Gym will allow you to build reinforcement learning models, compare their performance in a standardized setting, and keep track of updated versions. It will also allow others to track your work and your performance and compare it to their own if you choose to share it.

We will cover the following topics in this chapter:

- Understanding how the agent updates the Q-table and uses it to make decisions
- Adapting the appropriate Bellman equation to write an `argmax` function that updates the Q-table with each action
- Understanding the role of the learning parameters in the Bellman equation and what happens when they are adjusted
- Implementing epsilon decay to improve the performance of your agent

Technical requirements

You will need the following packages installed to complete the exercises in this chapter and the upcoming chapters:

- Python 3.5+ (we will be using Python 3.6 in this book)
- NumPy
- OpenAI Gym (see `Chapter 3`, *Setting Up Your First Environment with OpenAI Gym*, for installation and setup instructions)

 We strongly encourage you to familiarize yourself with the official OpenAI Gym documentation for the Taxi-v2 environment as well as the other environments we will be working with in this book. You will find a great deal of useful information on these environments and how to access the information and functionality you need from them. You can find the documentation at `https://gym.openai.com/docs/`.

The code for the exercises in this chapter can be found at `https://github.com/PacktPublishing/Hands-On-Q-Learning-with-Python/tree/master/Chapter04`.

Getting to know your learning agent

As we've seen in our exploration of the Taxi-v2 environment, your agent is a self-driving taxicab whose job it is to pick up passengers from a starting location and drop them off at their desired destination as efficiently as possible. The taxi collects a reward when it drops off a passenger and gets penalties for taking other actions. The following is a rendering of the taxi environment:

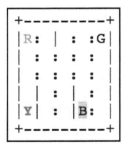

The rewards your agent collects are stored in the Q-table. The Q-table in our model-free algorithm is a lookup table that maps states to actions.

Think of the Q-table as an implementation of a Q-function of the Q form `(state, action)`. The function takes the state we are in and the actions we can take in that state and returns a Q-value. For our purposes, this will be the current highest-valued action the agent has already seen in that state.

 Remember that we will not always take the action with the highest Q-value. Depending on our explore-exploit strategy and the way we have chosen to decay epsilon, we might take a different, random action instead.

By the end of this chapter, you will have created a truly self-modifying AI agent. When your algorithm is complete, your agent will start out with no knowledge of the taxi environment and will quickly learn the rules that get it the highest rewards through exploration of the environment.

During this process, you will see your agent start to reach its goal more quickly and efficiently, and it will learn to do this without being explicitly programmed to do so. You will also be able to see its performance improve as it reaches the goal faster (in fewer time steps) as our implementation of the algorithm improves.

In discrete-state environments with relatively small state spaces, the Q-functions we write in the form of Q-tables will tend to converge relatively quickly, especially if we have implemented the required optimization function efficiently and modeled the state space well. The following is the sample Q-table:

Q-table initialised at zero

	UP	DOWN	LEFT	RIGHT
0	0	0	0	0
1	0	0	0	0
2	0	0	0	0
3	0	0	0	0
4	0	0	0	0
5	0	0	0	0
6	0	0	0	0
7	0	0	0	0
8	0	0	0	0

After few episodes

	UP	DOWN	LEFT	RIGHT
0	0	0	0	0
1	0	0	0	0
2	0	2.25	2.25	0
3	0	0	5	0
4	0	0	0	0
5	0	0	0	0
6	0	5	0	0
7	0	0	2.25	0
8	0	0	0	0

Eventually

	UP	DOWN	LEFT	RIGHT
0	0	0	0.45	0
1	0	1.01	0	0
2	0	2.25	2.25	0
3	0	0	5	0
4	0	0	0	0
5	0	0	0	0
6	0	5	0	0
7	0	0	2.25	0
8	0	0	0	0

In the preceding example, the last table shows what a sample Q-table will look like when it has converged or reached its final state. When this happens, updating the table will no longer change the Q-values.

The states are all initialized to zero, meaning that they have not yet been visited. When a state is visited and actions are taken from that state, we update the entry in the table to reflect the new value of that state-action pair. We'll go through this process in detail in later sections of this chapter, but, for now, it's enough to understand that the values in the table start at zero and will change as we progress through the task.

Notice that not all of the states in the preceding table have changed at all. This indicates that these states have not been visited (if the entire row of Q-values for those states remains at zero) or that the corresponding actions have not been taken from those states.

As mentioned, we will know that the Q-table has reached its final state when every time it gets updated with new Q-values, they are equal to its current values, so that, effectively, the table values stop changing and the function has converged. Once the Q-function has converged, we know that the environment has been solved and that the agent has found the optimal path to the goal.

In continuous-state environments, which might have infinite numbers of states, we are unlikely to see the function fully converge, even when we can calculate the conditions under which it should converge. Our goal when working with these environments will be to model the state-action function the agent is using during the training phase so we can generalize about states the agent has not yet seen.

The Q-learning implementation we'll create in this chapter is a model-free implementation. As we've discussed earlier, a model-free RL algorithm does not explicitly model its environment, or generate a state-action function that it uses to predict the Q-values of unseen states. Instead, it estimates the Q-values of these states and keeps improving on those estimates until the estimates converge and an optimal solution has been found.

Implementing your agent

Let's recreate the Taxi-v2 environment. We'll need to import `numpy` this time. We'll be using the term state instead of observation in this chapter for consistency with the terminology we used in Chapter 1, *Brushing Up on Reinforcement Learning Concepts*:

```
import gym
import numpy as np
env = gym.make('Taxi-v2')
state = env.reset()
```

Create the Q-table as follows:

```
Q = np.zeros([env.observation_space.n, env.action_space.n])
```

The Q-table is initialized as a two-dimensional numpy array of zeroes. The first three rows of the Q-table currently look like this:

State	South(0)	North(1)	East(2)	West(3)	Pickup(4)	Dropoff(5)
0	0	0	0	0	0	0
1	0	0	0	0	0	0
2	0	0	0	0	0	0

The first column represents the state, and the other column names represent the six possible actions. The Q-values for of all the state-action pairs are currently at zero. This is because the agent has no knowledge of its environment yet and is starting out as a blank slate that will need to learn as it goes.

The Q-table does not have to be initialized as an array of zeroes, and in many implementations, it starts as an array of high values that decrease as rewards and penalties are discovered. This can often improve performance in exploration/exploitation scenarios. For the examples in this book, we'll be initializing all of our tables with zeroes.

If we're in state 1 and decided to take action 2 (East), and the Q-value we calculate for this state-action pair is −1, we would update the Q-table this way:

State	South(0)	North(1)	East(2)	West(3)	Pickup(4)	Dropoff(5)
0	0	0	0	0	0	0
1	0	0	−1	0	0	0
2	0	0	0	0	0	0

That's it! That's how the Q-table is updated. (We'll step through this process in the next section in detail.)

When the learning agent returns to state 1 again, it will look up the row in the Q-table for state 1 to get the action values. When it does, it will see that the action with the lowest Q-value is currently action 2.

Let's see how this is accomplished in Python:

```
action = np.argmax(Q[state])
next_state, reward, done, info = env.step(action)
Q[state,action] = reward + gamma * np.max(Q[next_state])
```

The preceding three lines form the most crucial part of our code. Let's step through them.

`action = np.argmax(Q[state])` returns the index of the maximum value in the `<state>` row of the Q-table. Suppose state `100` of the Q-table looks like this:

State	South(0)	North(1)	Right(2)	Left(3)	Pickup(4)	Dropoff(5)
100	-1	0	-10	-1.618	-1	-10

The highest-valued action in this row is `North` (index `1`), with a value of `0`. If we called `np.argmax(Q[100])` at this point in the game loop, it would return `1`. Note that `np.argmax()` returns the `index` of the highest value (`1`), not the value itself (`0`).

In our current example, before we've taken any actions at all, the second row of the Q-table looks like this:

State	0	1	2	3	4	5
1	0	0	0	0	0	0

Let's see what happens when we run the following line:

```
action = np.argmax(Q[state])
```

All of the values in `Q[1]` are equal, so `np.argmax()` chooses the first of these values, which is `Q[1,0]`. The value stored in action is now `0` (`South`). Our current action is, therefore, to go one space south.

Once we've retrieved the value and stored it in `action`, we step through the environment with `env.step()` and take that action:

```
next_state, reward, done, info = env.step(action)
```

`next_state` now gives us the state we're in as a result of taking that action. Let's suppose it's state 2. We also now have a reward value. Let's assume that value is `-1`. This is the information we need to use to update the Q-table for the value of `Q[1,0]`.

We are updating the value of this state-action pair based on the highest Q-value of the action the agent could take from the next state. This is an essential characteristic of the Q-learning algorithm.

The value function – calculating the Q-value of a state-action pair

In this section, we'll go through how to update the Q-table by calculating the Q-value of the state we're in and the action we're taking.

As a learning agent, when we're in a state and decide to take an action, our job is to choose the optimal next action based on what we know about our situation so far. When we're at a corner and want to decide whether to turn right or left, we want to look back to the last time we were at that corner, and the time before that, and what happened when we made each decision.

Which decision yielded the highest rewards for us over time?

The Q-table is our agent's way of storing this information and calling it up again when it's needed. It is implemented as a lookup table, and it's your agent's way of rewriting its own code and modifying its own behavior as it runs. Let's step through this in detail.

Implementing Bellman equations

We're starting with a simplified Bellman equation for the first part of our code:

$$Q(s, a) = R(s, a) + \gamma[max(Q'(s', a'))]$$

Note that we are only including gamma in this equation at the moment. We'll include alpha and epsilon in later iterations. Let's assume we're choosing a value of `0.1` for gamma.

This is what that equation looks like in Python:

```
Q[state,action] = reward + gamma * np.max(Q[next_state])
```

If you're a Python programmer, but not a mathematician, this version is probably much less intimidating than the math version, but it works exactly the same way. Let's go through each part of this equation.

This is an assignment where we are setting the value of `Q[state, action]`:

- The variable reward on the right side gives us the reward for taking that action (the current value of `R[state, action]`, which is returned to us by Gym as the value reward)
- `np.max(Q[next_state])` tells us the highest valued-action we can take from the next state we would be in after taking the current action

This is what rows `Q[0]`, `Q[1]`, and `Q[2]` look like upon initialization:

State	0	1	2	3	4	5
0	0	0	0	0	0	0
1	0	0	0	0	0	0
2	0	0	0	0	0	0

In our current simplified example, we've started in state 1 and `np.argmax(Q[state])` has chosen action 0 (South) as the next action for us to take. We set `action` to this value as follows:

```
action = np.argmax(Q[state])
```

The value of `Q[state, action]` that will be set is, therefore, `Q[1, 0]`. Calling `env.step(action)` with the = 0 action returns the following:

```
next_state, reward, done, info = env.step(action)
```

- `next_state`: 2
- `reward`: -1
- `done`: False

(We're omitting the `info` value since we won't be making use of it here.)

We now have a value for `reward` and a value for `next_state` to plug into the Q-table update function as follows:

```
Q[state,action] = reward + gamma * np.max(Q[next_state])
```

`np.max(Q[2])` returns a value of 0, since all of the values in `Q[2]` are currently zero. The second term on the right then resolves to zero, and the right side becomes $-1 + 0 = -1$. `Q[1, 0]` and is hence assigned a value of -1:

State	0	1	2	3	4	5
0	0	0	0	0	0	0

| 1 | -1 | 0 | 0 | 0 | 0 | 0 |
| 2 | 0 | 0 | 0 | 0 | 0 | 0 |

Congratulations! We've just gone through a full update cycle of the Q-table by using the Bellman equation to calculate the highest Q-value of the state-action pair we're currently in.

The following is all of the code you'll need to get this preliminary version of your agent running. Notice that we're starting with a gamma value of `0.1`, and we haven't included alpha or epsilon yet:

```
import gym
import numpy as np

#create environment
env = gym.make("Taxi-v2")

#initialize Q-table
Q = np.zeros([env.observation_space.n, env.action_space.n])

#set hyperparameters
gamma = 0.1

#initialize reward
reward = 0

#initialize environment
state = env.reset()
```

First, we set up the environment and initialize the variables, then we create a game loop that exits when the goal state has been reached (when `reward = 20`). The game loop consists of the code we examined earlier:

- Get the current highest-valued action
- Retrieve the value of the next state we would be in if we took that action
- Update the Q-value of our current state-action pair using that value
- Update our current state to that next state

```
#create update loop
while reward != 20                   #while dropoff state has not been reached
    #choose current highest-valued action
    action = np.argmax(Q[state])

    #obtain reward and next state resulting from taking action
    next_state, reward, done, info = env.step(action)
```

```
        #update Q-value for state-action pair
        Q[state, action] = reward + gamma * np.max(Q[next_state])

        #update state
        state = next_state

    #render final dropoff state
    env.render()
```

The last line, `env.render()`, shows you the final state your agent is in after it completes the dropoff. But remember that we'd like more than just to be told the agent finally reached the goal. We want to know how many steps it took, what the rewards were, how the Q-table was updated, and so on, so that we can judge the performance of our model and improve on it.

Here's the result of running the preceding completed code:

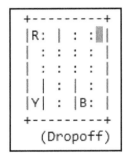

This is the last state the environment reaches, where the taxi has just dropped off its passenger (so the last action taken was **Dropoff**). As mentioned earlier, the taxi appears green since it was carrying a passenger during its last action.

Notice that we aren't taking any random actions here (which we would do if we were using epsilon). We're always selecting the action with the current highest Q-value. Effectively, we're using a simple greedy strategy.

Also, while we're updating the Q-table with the reward values we encounter (because we aren't doing any exploration at all), we are very likely to get stuck following the same paths over and over depending on where our initial random state is set.

Let's go back to our randomly-acting agent from the last chapter:

```
state = env.reset()
count = 0
reward = 0
while reward != 20:
```

```
    state, reward, done, info = env.step(env.action_space.sample())
env.render()
```

We're going to add in a counter to see how many steps this agent takes to reach the goal:

```
state = env.reset()
count = 0
reward = 0
while reward != 20:
    state, reward, done, info = env.step(env.action_space.sample())
    count += 1
env.render()
print('Counter: {}'.format(count))
```

The first time we ran this loop, we got a counter value of 1998, meaning the taxi took 1,998 random steps before it managed to pick up the passenger and drop them off at the correct location:

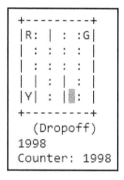

Running the loop multiple times gives similar results.

We can do the same for the simple Q-learning agent we just built:

```
Q = np.zeros([env.observation_space.n, env.action_space.n])
gamma = 0.1
state = env.reset()
count = 0
reward = 0
while reward != 20:
    action = np.argmax(Q[state])
    next_state, reward, done, info = env.step(action)
    Q[state, action] = reward + gamma * np.max(Q[next_state])
    state = next_state
    count += 1
env.render()
print('Counter: {}'.format(count))
```

Here's a typical result we got running the preceding loop:

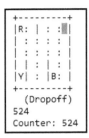

As part of your own research, you can set up an episode counter that will run multiple episodes and record the average time it takes for the randomly-acting agent to complete a successful **Dropoff**. You can do the same for the simple Q-learning agent and compare their performance.

Try it out and see what happens. Does the Q-learning agent perform better or worse on average than the randomly-acting agent? We'll also compare those versions of the taxi agent to the more advanced ones we will create in later sections.

The learning parameters – alpha, gamma, and epsilon

Here's an updated version of the Bellman equation:

$$Q * (s, a) = Q(s, a) + \propto [R(s, a) + \gamma[max(Q'(s', a'))] - Q(s, a)]$$

Compare it to the version we used in the last section:

$$Q(s, a) = R(s, a) + \gamma[max(Q'(s', a'))]$$

In the new version, we've added in an alpha term, which means we need to include the current Q-value of the state-action pair and discount it by the alpha value.

The first equation is telling us that the new Q-value (the right side of the equation) of our state-action pair is equal to the old Q-value plus the current reward and the discounted future reward, minus the old Q-value multiplied by the alpha term. Because the alpha value is relatively small, more of the current Q-value is incorporated into the new Q-value. In both versions of the equation, because the gamma value is also relatively small, current rewards are valued more highly than future rewards.

Notice that, if the alpha value is 1, the first equation reduces to the second, and we don't have to distinguish the new Q-value from the current one with a starred Q. This was exactly the equation we used in our first Q-learning algorithm.

Recall that an alpha value of 1 means we are treating an environment as totally deterministic so that, every time we take an action from a state, we end up in the same new state.

(On the opposite end of the scale, an alpha value of 0 would cause the agent to learn nothing at all. The second term in the first equation would disappear, and the new Q-values would always be the same as the old ones.)

In this case, we're going to choose a new value for alpha, such as 0.1. We're choosing this value for experimental purposes and not due to any knowledge of how the agent will behave with this alpha value.

Once we have tested and have additional knowledge of the effect of this alpha value and others, we will use that knowledge to choose future values. Additionally, once we've tested out multiple different ranges of values, we'll be able to take advantage of the results we get and not have to repeat the testing process.

Adding an updated alpha value

You will recall that alpha ranges from 0 to 1. An alpha value of 0 will have an agent learn nothing, and an alpha value of 1 will have it learn policies completely specific to a deterministic environment.

It can sometimes be to our advantage to decay alpha as a task progresses, because there might be less that we need to learn about it as we progress. A high alpha value can, in some situations, lead to overfitting, or learning overly specific lessons about an environment, and decaying alpha can help to prevent that.

Here's our code from the previous section, updated with a new alpha value:

```
Q = np.zeros([env.observation_space.n, env.action_space.n])
gamma = 0.1
alpha = 0.1
state = env.reset()
count = 0
reward = 0
while reward != 20:
    action = np.argmax(Q[state])
    next_state, reward, done, info = env.step(action)
```

```
        Q[state, action] = Q[state, action] + alpha * (reward + gamma *   \
                           np.max(Q[next_state]) - Q[state, action])
        state = next_state
        count += 1
env.render()
print('Counter: {}'.format(count))
```

You will notice the format of our new Bellman equation:

```
Q[state, action] = Q[state, action] + alpha * (reward + gamma *   \
                   np.max(Q[next_state]) - Q[state, action])
```

We see that this is a direct translation into Python of the first Bellman equation. Because this is an assignment, we know that the current Q-value of the associated `state` and `action` variables will be used to assign the new Q-value. Notice that, in an equation, we have to distinguish the current value from the updated value using a `Q*` designation.

Test out the new version of this code and see whether you get improved results from the previous two iterations of your taxi agent. What is the average number of steps it takes for this new version of the algorithm to reach the destination?

Adding an updated epsilon value

The last hyperparameter we want to add in is epsilon, so that our agent has the ability to explore new actions it hasn't taken yet and balance out its exploitation of the high-valued actions it's already taken. (For more detail on this, refer back to the exploration versus exploitation sections in Chapter 1, *Brushing Up on Reinforcement Learning Concepts*, and Chapter 2, *Getting Started with the Q-Learning Algorithm*.)

First, we choose an `epsilon` value between 0 and 1, say 0.1. We'll test and compare different values for epsilon as part of our model-tuning process.

We add the `epsilon` value to our algorithm and add a condition to the game loop to modify the way we choose actions:

```
Q = np.zeros([env.observation_space.n, env.action_space.n])
gamma = 0.1
alpha = 0.1
epsilon = 0.1
state = env.reset()
count = 0
reward = 0
```

We now choose a random number between 0 and 1, and if that number is less than epsilon, we take a random action. Otherwise, we take the highest Q-valued action as before:

```
while reward != 20:

    if np.random.rand() < epsilon:

        #exploration option
        action = env.action_space.sample()

    else:
        #exploitation option
        action = np.argmax(Q[state])
```

That's the only change we have to make! We've now incorporated exploration into our agent's decision-making process and can benefit from choosing new actions and lower the risk of getting stuck on local maxima.

We will update the Q-table and continue the task loop as before:

```
    next_state, reward, done, info = env.step(action)
    Q[state, action] = Q[state, action] + alpha * (reward + gamma *  \
                        np.max(Q[next_state]) - Q[state, action])

    state = next_state
    count += 1

env.render()
print('Counter: {}'.format(count))
```

We can change and test out different values of epsilon as needed and see which values give us the best performance.

Model-tuning and tracking your agent's long-term performance

As we build and tune our models, we need to test their performance and make sure they are improving with respect to speed and accuracy. In general, a model that performs better as it is fed more data is a model that is fitted well to its training environment. Let's test the performance of our baseline agent against our learning model and observe what happens when we run the model over more iterations.

Comparing your models and statistical performance measures

Let's go back to our randomly-acting baseline agent. We've changed the variable name, count, to epochs to distinguish each training time step from each full game loop cycle the agent completes:

```
state = env.reset()
epochs = 0
reward = 0

while reward != 20:
    state, reward, done, info = env.step(env.action_space.sample())
    epochs += 1
env.render()

print("Timesteps taken: {}".format(epochs))
```

As our first step in testing our results and comparing them to the output of other models, we're going to add in an episode loop that will make this agent run through the game loop 100 times and keep track of the results each time. We want to find the average number of steps it takes the agent to reach the destination each time it starts from the beginning:

```
total_epochs = 0
episodes = 100

for episode in range(episodes):
    epochs = 0
    reward = 0
    state = env.reset()

    while reward != 20:
        action = env.action_space.sample()
```

```
        state, reward, done, info = env.step(action)
        epochs += 1
    total_epochs += epochs

print("Average timesteps taken: {}".format(total_epochs/episodes))
```

We calculate the average number of time steps by dividing the total number of epochs per game iteration (time step) by the total number of episodes (number of game iterations run), as follows:

```
total_epochs = 0
episodes = 100

for episode in range(0, episodes):
    epochs = 0
    reward = 0
    state = env.reset()
    while reward != 20:
        action = env.action_space.sample()
        state, reward, done, info = env.step(action)
        epochs += 1
    total_epochs += epochs
print("Average timesteps taken: {}".format(total_epochs/episodes))

Average timesteps taken: 2464.7
```

The first time we run this loop, we get an average number of 2464.7 time steps, and running it a few times gives us similar results. You should see results close to this when you run this simulation yourself.

As we'll find out when we compare it to our learning models, the randomly-acting agent is performing very poorly for this environment. We don't want it taking thousands of steps and making many wrong moves before managing to drop the passenger off at the correct location. As of now, it can't keep track of anything it has seen so far or learn from any of its experiences.

Let's bring Q-learning into the picture:

```
Q = np.zeros([env.observation_space.n, env.action_space.n])

gamma = 0.1
alpha = 0.1
epsilon = 0.1
total_epochs = 0
episodes = 100

for episode in range(episodes):
    epochs = 0
    reward = 0
    state = env.reset()

    while reward != 20:
        if np.random.rand() < epsilon:
            action = env.action_space.sample()
        else:
            action = np.argmax(Q[state])
        next_state, reward, done, info = env.step(action)
        Q[state, action] = Q[state, action] + alpha * (reward + gamma * \
                            np.max(Q[next_state]) - Q[state, action])
        state = next_state
        epochs += 1
    total_epochs += epochs

print("Average timesteps taken: {}".format(total_epochs/episodes))

Average timesteps taken: 663.97
```

Even after running just 100 episodes, we're already doing better than the randomly-acting agent. The agent is now averaging 663.97 time steps to reach the goal.

Let's try some tweaks to see how our performance improves.

Training your models

What happens if we run the random agent for more episodes? Let's try 10000 episodes instead of 100 (warning: depending on your machine, this may take a long time to run!):

```
total_epochs = 0
episodes = 10000

for episode in range(episodes):
    epochs = 0
    reward = 0
    state = env.reset()
    while reward != 20:
        action = env.action_space.sample()
        state, reward, done, info = env.step(action)
        epochs += 1
    total_epochs += epochs
print("Average timesteps taken: {}".format(total_epochs/episodes))

Average timesteps taken: 2255.7757
```

This doesn't help at all. The random agent can't learn from its actions, and no matter how many times we try to run it, it will never get any better at the task. But, what about the learning agent? Let's have a look:

```
Q = np.zeros([env.observation_space.n, env.action_space.n])

gamma = 0.1
alpha = 0.1
epsilon = 0.1
total_epochs = 0
episodes = 10000

for episode in range(episodes):
    epochs = 0
    reward = 0
    state = env.reset()

    while reward != 20:
        if np.random.rand() < epsilon:
            action = env.action_space.sample()
        else:
            action = np.argmax(Q[state])
        next_state, reward, done, info = env.step(action)
        Q[state, action] = Q[state, action] + alpha * (reward + gamma * \
                        np.max(Q[next_state]) - Q[state, action])
        state = next_state
        epochs += 1
    total_epochs += epochs

print("Average timesteps taken: {}".format(total_epochs/episodes))

Average timesteps taken: 46.0174
```

Excellent. The learning agent has improved its performance more than tenfold with the increased training. This loop should also run much faster than the random agent loop, since the learning agent has to take progressively fewer steps as its performance improves.

What happens when you increase the number of episodes to `100000`? Does the agent's performance get better or worse, or does it stay the same? Try it out for yourself (note that this could also take a long time to run).

Decaying epsilon

As we learn more and more about our environment and find out where the high-valued actions are, we want to do more exploitation of those high-valued actions and less exploration of other potential actions that we may not have discovered yet. There are several ways to decay epsilon and improve the performance of our model.

One option we can use is to decay epsilon in a straight line, independent of the values in the Q-table. That's the option we'll be using at first:

```python
Q = np.zeros([env.observation_space.n, env.action_space.n])
gamma = 0.1
alpha = 0.1
epsilon = 0.1
epsilon_decay = 0.99 #decay factor

total_epochs = 0
episodes = 10000

for episode in range(episodes):
    epochs = 0
    reward = 0
  epsilon = epsilon * epsilon_decay #decay step

    state = env.reset()
```

Each time the game loop runs, the value of epsilon decreases by `1%`. Does this improve the performance of your model? Test out different values of epsilon decay to see the effects:

```python
    while reward != 20:

        if np.random.rand() < epsilon:
            action = env.action_space.sample()
        else:
            action = np.argmax(Q[state])
        next_state, reward, done, info = env.step(action)
        Q[state, action] = Q[state, action] + alpha * (reward + gamma * \
```

```
                           np.max(Q[next_state]) - Q[state, action])
        state = next_state
        epochs += 1
        total_epochs += epochs

    print("Average timesteps taken: {}".format(total_epochs/episodes))
```

As we progress through this book, we'll learn that there are other ways to decay epsilon that aren't based on an arbitrary constant but are based on the values produced by the model itself, such as the Q-values.

Often, it can be to our advantage to have our value of epsilon adjust based on the level of exploration we've already done, as this will often limit or constrain the exploration we want to do in the future. There are several strategies for decaying epsilon that make use of this observation. We'll discuss them in detail in `Chapter 8`, *Further Q-Learning Research and Future Projects*, in our exploration of multi-armed bandits.

Hyperparameter tuning

In later chapters, we'll discuss methods for how to choose optimal values for alpha, gamma, and epsilon in more detail. For now, we'll use the values we have and test different values against each other manually. One of the most straightforward options is a cross-validation method, such as a grid search, which can be done programmatically.

Recall that hyperparameter tuning in machine learning is the process of finding the hyperparameters for a model (such as the depth or number of nodes of a decision tree) that will get the best performance for that model:

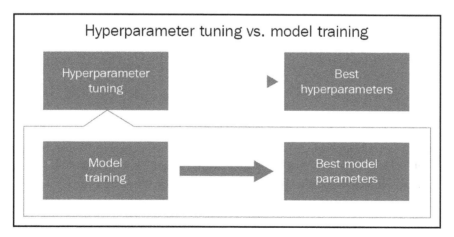

As we mentioned earlier, the hyperparameter values are not determined by the model itself. You can think of them as independent variables that are controlled by outside sources, in this case, the decisions made by the researcher designing the model.

As part of the tuning process, we generally try out different values for the hyperparameters to see which ones allow the model to learn optimally and produce the best results. Sometimes an optimal value of a hyperparameter might be widely-known in the RL research community (for example, many examples you'll see for the taxi environment will use a value close to 0.6 for gamma). This is another benefit of being able to learn from and compare your work to the results of other researchers.

In the case of Q-learning, the hyperparameters that can be tuned are alpha, gamma, and epsilon, as well as any decay factors we apply to these hyperparameters. When we're constructing models as part of this book, we'll discuss what values of the three hyperparameters we've chosen to use and give a rationale for these values.

Summary

In this chapter, we've created, trained, and tested our first Q-learning agent. We've seen how a version of the Bellman equation works and we translated it into Python using an `argmax` function to calculate the Q-value of a state-action pair.

We trained and tested our learning agent against our random agent and compared their performances. We saw that the longer the learning agent is trained, the more it learns about its environment and the better it performs at finding an optimal solution.

In the next chapter, we'll explore problems where the state space is too complex to use a Q-table. We'll use neural networks, and, later, deep learning structures called deep Q-networks, to approximate Q-values. We'll also explore several different Python packages used for building neural networks and compare the merits of each one.

Questions

1. Why do we choose to use the words state and observation interchangeably? When would be a more appropriate time to use the word state?
2. How do we know when the Q-function has converged?
3. What happens to the Q-table when the Q-function has converged?
4. When do we know the agent has found the optimal path to the goal? Describe in terms of the previous two questions.

5. What does `numpy.argmax()` return?
6. What does `numpy.max()` return?
7. Why does the randomly-acting agent take thousands of time steps to reach the goal? How does the Q-learning agent perform better?
8. Describe one benefit of decaying alpha.
9. What is overfitting and how does it apply in the context of an RL model?
10. By what order of magnitude does the number of time steps needed to reach the goal reduce when the number of training episodes is multiplied by 10? Give a general response to this; there may be multiple valid answers depending on the parameters you use.
11. Explain in two to three sentences how the agent chooses an action based on the value of epsilon and what happens when we decay epsilon.
12. When do we need to use neural networks or deep learning with a Q-learning problem?

Section 2: Building and Optimizing Q-Learning Agents

We will learn how to build more advanced Q-learning models by combining Q-learning with deep learning and giving the agent an existing model of a problem to work from. We will learn the challenges of reinforcement learning in an environment with sparse data and will work with delayed returns. The reader will become familiar with implementing deep Q-networks to solve problems and learn about the different challenges they can be used to address.

The following chapters are included in this section:

- Chapter 5, *Building Q-Networks with TensorFlow*
- Chapter 6, *Digging Deeper into Deep Q-Networks with Keras and TensorFlow*

5
Building Q-Networks with TensorFlow

As the number of states in a Q-learning task increases, a simple Q-table is no longer a practical way of modeling the state-action transition function. Instead, we will use a Q-network, which is a type of neural network that is designed to approximate Q-values.

Approximating Q-values allows us to build a model of a Q-learning task that maps states to actions. In this chapter, we will discuss how neural networks can be used to recognize states and map these to actions, which allows us to approximate Q-values instead of using a lookup table.

We'll understand what a policy agent is in comparison to a value agent, which we implemented in the previous chapter. In addition to discussing how the network we build adjusts to model the problem that we're working with, we'll also learn more about Q-networks at a higher level.

We will cover the following topics in this chapter:

- A brief overview of neural networks
- Implementing a neural network with NumPy
- Neural networks and Q-learning
- Building your first Q-network

Technical requirements

You will need the following packages installed to complete the exercises in this chapter:

- Python 3.5+
- NumPy
- OpenAI Gym (you can refer to `Chapter 3`, *Setting Up Your First Environment with OpenAI Gym*, for installation and setup instructions)
- TensorFlow

 We strongly encourage you to familiarize yourself with the official OpenAI Gym documentation for the Taxi-v2 environment and other environments that we will be working with in this book. You will find a great deal of useful information on these environments including how to access the functionality that you need from them. You can find the documentation at `https://gym.openai.com/docs/`.

You can access the code files for this chapter at `https://github.com/PacktPublishing/Hands-On-Q-Learning-with-Python/tree/master/Chapter05`.

A brief overview of neural networks

Broadly speaking, a neural network is a type of machine learning framework that is built for pattern-matching. Neural networks are often used to classify input data, such as images or text, based on the extensional definitions of the type of object they are identifying. A classifier network, for example, might be given images as input and labels as output, and then use this to determine an internal function that will map the **Inputs** to the **Outputs**:

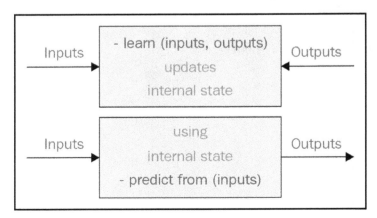

The first black box operation in the preceding diagram indicates that the network is being trained and is updating its approximation of the input and output function based on incoming data. The second box represents the testing process, where the network uses its internal function to make predictions on new incoming data.

Think of the way a machine learning algorithm, such as a decision tree classifier, takes in feature columns and a target column from a data table and creates a function using the feature columns that will predict the target column. A neural network accomplishes the same task, but the feature columns it uses are internal to the network and not explicitly accessible to us. The inputs it receives might be in the form of images or text to analyze, for example. In other words, the neural network has to create the feature columns itself.

Let's review some concepts related to neural networks before we dive into the specifics of Q-networks.

Extensional versus intensional definitions

An **extensional definition** is a definition that is given in examples, as opposed to an **intensional** or "dictionary" definition. An extensional definition of the word "car" might be various labeled images of cars, along with labeled images of objects that are not cars.

A neural network trained on these images should be able to identify new images that are not in the training set as belonging to either the "car" or "not car" class. Once it has accomplished this with a level of accuracy that is useful for the purposes we are putting it to, we can say that it has learned to define what a car is.

By contrast, an intensional definition of "car" might be "a four-wheeled vehicle powered by an internal combustion engine." This is also what we think of as a dictionary definition.

Neural networks learn to classify inputs by using extensional definitions of these inputs, that is, by being trained on many examples of those inputs and learning what they have in common.

Taking a closer look

Let's examine the structure and operation of a simple neural network. This will only be a brief overview and will serve as a transition to the deep Q-network that we will be constructing later in this chapter. If you are already familiar with how basic networks and activation functions work, feel free to skip to the *Building your first deep Q-network* section.

We will not be doing an exhaustive primer on neural networks, but it's worth researching them further and becoming familiar with the basic concepts of propagating values through layers to make predictions and backpropagating errors to update the network based on the results. We'll provide an overview of this process here.

Input, hidden, and output layers

A simple neural network, such as a classifier, might consist of an input layer, a hidden layer, and an output layer. Each layer has a set of weights associated with it.

The values in the input layer of the network propagate through the network. The basis for calculating the node values of a new layer is by taking the dot product of the input and the network weights:

$$output = \sum (weights.\, inputs) + bias$$

The output is a matrix of prediction values. As with any machine learning classifier, the range of values is based on the number of classes. For a binary classifier, for example, the output values will be 0 or 1.

The goal of the network is to determine the correct values for the weights that will give it the best possible predictions for the true output values. This is where the machine learning component comes in.

In our simple network example, we'll use a method called **gradient descent** to take the network's errors in making its predictions (called the **loss**) and propagate it back through the network to update the values of the weights.

We calculate the values for the hidden layer by taking the dot product of the input layer and the network weights. Note that the dot product is a linear algebra operation on two matrices, X and Y:

$$X.\, Y = |X||Y| \cos(\theta)$$

Getting accurate outputs for each layer depends on the weight values being correct. When we first initialize the network, it does not know what the correct weight values are, so it has to make guesses and correct its assumptions when it compares its predictions to the real values. This process is called backpropagation, and we'll see how that works later.

Perceptron functions

The simplest kind of neural network to understand is a binary classifier called the perceptron. The following diagram is an overview of how the perceptron works:

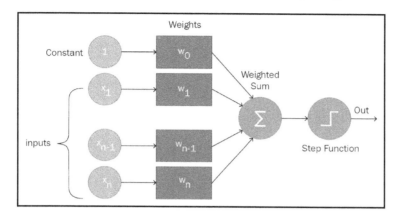

We see that the **inputs** are coming in and being multiplied by the weights, and then an overall weighted sum is taken:

$$output = \sum(weights.\,input)$$

This is the process of taking the dot product of two matrices or vectors. The values at the weighted sum node are then sent to an activation function called a **step function**

An activation function effectively maps inputs onto outputs and determines what the outputs will be. In case of this unit step function, it returns **0** if x is negative or **1** if x is positive.

We can think of an activation function as determining whether an individual node will fire (return 1) or not (return 0), in the same way that a neuron in a human brain will fire and transmit its output to another neuron.

The following equation is of a neuron which has the input $(x_1\text{-}x_n)$, their corresponding weights $(w_1\text{-}w_n)$, a bias (b), and the activation function (f) applied to the weighted sum of the inputs:

$$f\left(b + \sum_{i=1}^{n} x_i w_i\right)$$

The outputs of the step function are the results of our binary classifier.

There are a number of activation functions that we'll become familiar with in our study and practice of building neural networks, such as the sigmoid, tanh, and **Rectified Linear Unit (ReLU)** functions:

- The following diagram illustrates a **sigmoid** function:

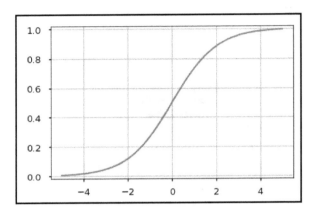

- The following diagram illustrates a **tanh** function:

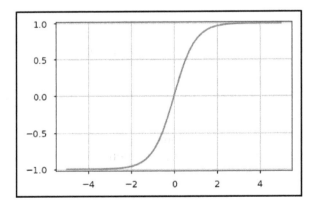

- The following diagram illustrates a **ReLU** function:

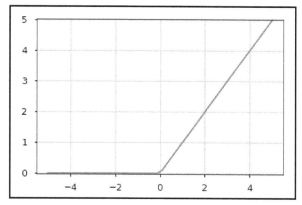

The ReLU function is the most commonly-used activation function in neural networks and it is a good function to start building with. Let's take a look at how to implement it.

ReLU functions

A ReLU function is a type of activation function. As previously discussed, an activation function provides the output of a node in a network (such as 0 or 1). In the case of a ReLU function, our outputs will be a wider range of integer values.

Here is a very simple implementation of a ReLU function:

```
def ReLU(x):
    if x > 0:
        return x
    return 0
```

For an input x, the ReLU function returns x if x is positive, and 0 if it is not. The ReLU is unbounded on the right-side and can go to infinity. Effectively, the ReLU is flattening the negative inputs to zero and only keeping the positive inputs.

We won't need to implement an actual ReLU function ourselves in this way; the function will be packaged into a framework such as TensorFlow for us. Now that we're familiar with how the nuts and bolts of the function work, we can zoom out and focus on larger-scale operations.

Any neural network implementation package that we use, such as TensorFlow, will provide a data structure called a tensor. Conceptually, a tensor has the same structure as a NumPy array, but it can keep track internally of computation gradients and utilize GPUs for faster operation. In comparison, a NumPy array has no built-in ability to do this.

Before we get into a tensor-based implementation, let's first explore how to make use of the NumPy framework to manually implement a forward pass and backpropagation process for a three-layer neural network.

Implementing a neural network with NumPy

In this section, we are implementing a fully-connected ReLU classifier using NumPy.

Note that, in practice, we wouldn't implement a simple neural network with this level of detail; this is only for demonstration purposes so that we can get comfortable with the matrix multiplication and feedforward structure that is involved.

As mentioned in the previous section, NumPy has no internal structure for handling gradients or computation graphs; it is a broadly-used framework within Python for scientific computing. However, we can apply matrix operations to NumPy objects to simulate a two-layer network that incorporates feedforward and backpropagation.

 All of the code for this section can be found in the GitHub repository for this chapter; note that not all of the code is published here.

We begin by importing the required package, as follows:

```
import numpy as np
```

We create some random input and output data:

```
x = np.random.randn(n, d_in)
y = np.random.randn(n, d_out)
```

Effectively, we are going to give this set of input and output data to a neural network and ask it to find a **function** that will relate the inputs to the output data.

We initialize the network weights, as follows:

```
weights_1 = np.random.randn(d_in, hidden_layer)
weights_2 = np.random.randn(hidden_layer, d_out)
```

Right now, we are setting random values as the weights. As we train the network, it will update these weights so that they get progressively closer to the true function relating x to y.

Feedforward

We calculate the values for the hidden layer nodes by taking the dot product of the input layer, x, and the first set of weights, $w1$. We apply the ReLU function to the hidden layer, h, and store the result in `h_relu`, as follows:

```
...
h = x.dot(weights_1)
h_relu = np.maximum(h, 0)
```

Finally, we calculate our predicted y values by taking the dot product of the hidden layer and the second set of weights, $w2$:

```
y_pred = h_relu.dot(weights_2)
...
```

We now have a vector of predictions. Let's find out how good our predictions were by computing the loss function.

Backpropagation

We use the sum of squares formula to compute the loss function, as follows:

$$loss = \sum (y - y_{pred})2$$

Here, y - y_{pred} is the difference between the predicted and actual outputs.

We can implement it as follows:

```
loss = np.square(y_pred - y).sum()
```

We're now calculating the gradient descent with respect to the loss function. The gradient of a function, such as the derivative, is the slope of the tangent of the graph of that function.

Gradient descent finds the steepest slope and adjusts the weights according to that slope:

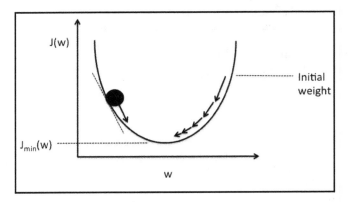

The preceding diagram makes gradient descent easier to understand intuitively. In the diagram, we check the slope (or gradient) of the point where the weight (that is, the black ball) is at each point.

Our goal is to get the slope to zero and to the lowest error level:

- If the slope is negative, the error will decrease if we increase the weight (that is, move right in the x direction).
- If the slope is positive, the error will decrease if we decrease the weight (that is, move left in the x direction).
- If the slope is 0, the error is already at the minimum level.

We multiply each loss term by a gradient value and obtain a gradient vector to recalculate the weights. Notice that we're moving from the outer layer to the inner layer, which is why we call this process backpropagation:

```
grad_y_pred = 2.0 * (y_pred - y)

grad_weights_2 = h_relu.T.dot(grad_y_pred)

grad_h_relu = grad_y_pred.dot(weights_2.T)

  . . .
```

Finally, we scale the weight values by the gradient vectors that we've calculated:

```
weights_1 -= learning_rate * grad_weights_1
weights_2 -= learning_rate * grad_weights_2
```

The network now has new weight values calculated based on the loss from its previous predictions. It has learned from its experience and is in a position to make more accurate predictions on the next set of test data.

Neural networks and Q-learning

When the state space for an environment gets too big, a Q-table is no longer a practical way in which to model the transition function between states and actions. Neural networks can help us to approximate the Q-value of a state, so that we don't need to use a lookup table to find the exact recorded function value.

One popular way to train a Q-network is to give it images that represent states. The network then looks at the actions that are possible in each state and predicts which action will yield the highest value if taken from that state. Generally, it is not looking at an exact Q-value in a table but at a probability distribution of values. We'll explore this type of network in the next chapter, after we learn about the basics of building Q-networks.

Policy agents versus value agents

Let's discuss one primary difference between the model-free agent that we built in `Chapter 4`, *Teaching a Smartcab to Drive Using Q-Learning*, and the Q-networks we'll be building here and in the next chapter. We've brought up this topic briefly before, but it's important to understand it at a higher level:

- Model-free Q-learning agents are **value agents**; they do not attempt to model the agent's policy or state-action function. They only represent the actual Q-values in their implementation, such as in a Q-table.
- **Policy agents**, such as the ones we'll be implementing with deep Q-networks, model the agent's policy:

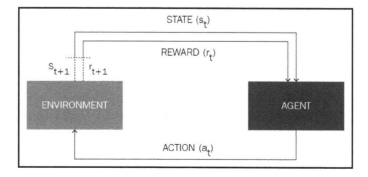

The primary practical difference is that policy agents, unlike value agents, develop the ability to generalize about an environment. They can then make predictions about states they have not yet seen.

Building your first Q-network

We are using the TensorFlow framework to build a Q-network that will solve the Taxi-v2 task. Note that this is a **single-layer network**, so it does not qualify as a deep Q-network. We'll be building a deep Q-network implementation in the next chapter.

 Many people use the term "deep learning" in association with any machine learning model that uses neural networks, and, in fact, some incorrectly generalize the term "deep Q-network" to include any Q-learning implementation that uses a neural network. The main distinction is that deep learning structures contain many hierarchical neural network layers that are constructed into various architectures.

The primary difference here from the model-free version that we built in Chapter 4, *Teaching a Smartcab to Drive Using Q-Learning*, is that, instead of updating a Q-table with the exact Q-values we encounter, we'll be using a neural network to approximate the Q-function that maps states to actions. We use a loss function to backpropagate and update the values of the weights in our approximation of the Q-function.

Bear in mind that the nodes in a neural network graph are the same structure as the tensors in the TensorFlow framework. Tensors are implemented as array objects with built-in properties and functions that allow many operations to be performed on them quickly and efficiently. We'll often use the words **tensor** and **node** to refer to the same kind of object in a network.

In high-level terms, the process we're carrying out is as follows:

- Taking the states as inputs to the network
- Predicting the Q-values for each action
- Computing the loss for each prediction
- Backpropagating the losses back through the network by updating the weights

This is very similar to what we do in the model-free version of Q-learning, where we take the current highest Q-valued action, look at the next set of actions we could take, and update the current Q-value based on the highest potential reward we could get. We are taking a step forward, evaluating our new position, and taking a step back to update our Q-value for our current position based on that new position.

The primary difference here is that the neural network is modeling the actual function linking states to actions, whereas in the model-free version, as the name suggests, we don't construct a model of this function and, instead, assume that the agent is always taking the optimal action from each state. At each update step, the Q-network gets closer to approximating the actual Q-function.

Defining the network

We first initialize the input layer using the `tf.placeholder()` function. We call this tensor a placeholder because its value hasn't been assigned yet.

Using a placeholder lets us build the structure of our computation graph without having the data yet. The results of evaluating this node will be fed into the output layer using the `feed_dict()` argument when the training session is run.

The state value is encoded as a one-hot vector of the shape, `[1, observation_space]`. We can get the length of the observation space with `env.observation_space.n`, as follows:

```
tf.reset_default_graph()

inputs = tf.placeholder(shape[1,env.observation_space.n], \
                    dtype=tf.float32)
```

We initialize the weights as a vector of the size, `[observation_space, action_space]`. We compute the output layer by taking the dot product of the input layer and the weights, as we have done previously. Similar to `observation_space`, we get the length of `action_space` with `env.action_space.n`.

As with our model-free version using the Q-table, our predictions are taken as the maximum of the current Q-values. We will backpropagate through the network and update the weights when we get the actual Q-value of taking the next action:

```
weights =
tf.Variable(tf.random_uniform([env.observation_space.n,env.action_space.n],
0, 0.01))

q_out = tf.matmul(inputs, weights)
predict = tf.argmax(q_out,1)
```

The `next_Q` value, like the input layer, is of the type, `tf.placeholder`, which means that it can be fed in as a value to another node but not evaluated. Effectively, it's a variable that we are not assigning a value to yet but are using to build the computation graph for the network. It will be utilized by the `feed_dict()` function in the training loop.

We compute the loss for our predictions by taking the sum of squares difference between the target and prediction Q-values, just as we did in the NumPy implementation of the ReLU function:

```
next_Q = tf.placeholder(shape=[1,env.action_space.n],dtype=tf.float32)

loss = tf.reduce_sum(tf.square(next_Q - Q_output))
trainer = tf.train.GradientDescentOptimizer(learning_rate=0.1)
updateModel = trainer.minimize(loss)
```

The gradient descent operation is carried out by the built-in TensorFlow `GradientDescentOptimizer()` function. As shown in the preceding code, the model is updated using the learning rate and loss function that we specify. The optimizer is set to minimize the loss function.

Training the network

Once we've defined the network, let's start training it as follows:

```
init = tf.global_variables_initializer()
total_epochs = 0
total_rewards  = 0

gamma = .7
epsilon = 0.2
epsilon_decay = 0.99
episodes = 2000
```

We choose the starting values for the hyperparameters and the number of episodes that we want to train for. The longer we train this model, the better its performance should be.

We're also using `total_epochs` and `total_rewards` to keep track of the timesteps that the network takes for each task cycle and the rewards it collects each time.

We start a session and initialize the task loop, as follows:

```
with tf.Session() as sess:
    sess.run(init)

    for episode in range(episodes):
```

```
state = env.reset()
rewards_this_episode = 0
done = False
epochs = 0
```

We've reset the preceding environment and initialized a new state.

We then use the `pred` function defined in the previous section to choose the current highest Q-valued action. We also have a chance of choosing a random action that is equal to epsilon:

```
while not done:
    action, q = sess.run([predict,q_out], feed_dict=
{inputs:np.identity(env.observation_space.n)[state:state + 1]})

    if np.random.rand(1) < epsilon:
        action[0] = env.action_space.sample()
    next_state, reward, done, info = env.step(action[0])
```

The `feed_dict` argument lets us plug the values for inputs into the prediction and output functions and compute the next action value. We then choose a random value and assign a random action if the value is less than epsilon.

Finally, we find the Q-values of the next state and obtain the maximum Q-value from that state to backpropagate through the network:

```
curr_q = sess.run(q_out, feed_dict =
{inputs:np.identity(env.observation_space.n)[next_state:next_state+1]})

max_next_q = np.max(curr_q)
target_q = q

#update Q-values

target_q[0, action[0]] = reward + gamma * max_next_q
```

We feed the target values back through the network to update the weights. We then set the current state to the `next_state` value to implement the chosen action value and continue through the task.

With this method, we are effectively approximating what the Q-value is for a state, finding out the actual Q-value, and correcting our approximation through updating the network weights. With a Q-table, we store actual values in a table, while with a Q-network, we store this information in the weights, which act as coefficients in the Q-function that maps states to actions:

```
info, new_weights = sess.run([loss_update, weights],
feed_dict={inputs:np.identity(env.observation_space.n)[state:state+1],
next_q:target_q})
rewards_this_episode += reward
state = next_state
epochs += 1
```

When we reach `done = true`, we decay the value of epsilon and exit the loop.

Decaying epsilon at this point will give us a reduced value the next time we run the task. This means that we will have a lower chance of exploration the longer we run the training loop:

```
epsilon = epsilon * epsilon_decay

#Decay epsilon and tabulate rewards for the round

total_epochs += epochs
total_rewards += rewards_this_episode
print ("Success rate: " + str(total_rewards/episodes))
```

We calculate the rewards per episode as a performance metric for our network. What fraction of rewards per episode does your implementation achieve when you run this task?

Summary

We've learned how neural networks work on a basic level and how to implement a simple network using NumPy. We learned about computing loss functions, gradient descent, and backpropagation to update the weights of a network and fit its internal function to a useful model of a dataset. We built our first Q-network using TensorFlow and gained an understanding of using the framework.

In the next chapter, we'll discuss how to improve on the Q-network that we built using methods such as experience replay and using images as input to a network. We'll be building a deep Q-network using Keras running on a TensorFlow backend. You can think of Keras as a wrapper or frontend for TensorFlow; it abstracts many of the functions that TensorFlow provides into an easy framework for building complex deep learning architectures.

Questions

1. What is the difference between an extensional and an intensional definition?
2. Define the concept of feedforward in a neural network.
3. Explain what role the weights play in a neural network. How is an input value propagated through the network?
4. Briefly describe gradient descent.
5. Briefly describe backpropagation.
6. Describe the difference between a policy agent and a value agent.
7. What is the difference between a tensor and an array? What benefit do we get from using tensors?
8. What is a placeholder tensor?
9. How does a Q-network update its internal approximation of the Q-values of a state-action function?
10. What types of architectures qualify as deep Q-networks?
11. Briefly describe the difference between a neural network that implements a Q-learning algorithm and a deep Q-network.

Further reading

- *A Beginner's Guide to Deep Reinforcement Learning*: https://skymind.ai/wiki/deep-reinforcement-learning
- *Parametrized Deep Q-Networks Learning: Reinforcement Learning with Discrete-Continuous Hybrid Action Space*: https://arxiv.org/abs/1810.06394

6
Digging Deeper into Deep Q-Networks with Keras and TensorFlow

In this chapter, we're going to build a deep Q-network to solve the well-known CartPole (inverted pendulum) problem. We'll be working with the OpenAI Gym CartPole-v1 environment. We'll also use Keras with a TensorFlow backend to implement our deep Q-network architecture.

We'll become familiar with OpenAI Gym's CartPole-v1 task and design a basic **Deep Q Learning (DQN)** structure. We'll construct our deep learning architecture using Keras and start to tune the learning parameters and add in epsilon decay to optimize the model. We'll also add in experience replay to improve our performance. At each iteration of our model-building process, we'll run a new training loop to observe the updated results.

The following topics will be covered in this chapter:

- Getting started with the CartPole task
- Building a DQN to solve the CartPole problem
- Testing and results
- Adding in experience replay
- Building further on DQNs

Technical requirements

You will need the following packages installed to complete the exercises in this chapter and upcoming chapters:

- Python 3.5+
- NumPy
- OpenAI Gym (see `Chapter 3`, *Setting Up Your First Environment with OpenAI Gym*, for installation and setup instructions)
- TensorFlow
- Keras

 We strongly encourage you to familiarize yourself with the official OpenAI Gym documentation for the Taxi-v2 environment as well as the other environments we will be working with in this book. You will find a great deal of useful information on these environments and how to access the information and functionality you need from them. You can find the documentation here: `https://gym.openai.com/docs/`.

You can find the code files for this chapter in the following link: `https://github.com/PacktPublishing/Hands-On-Q-Learning-with-Python/tree/master/Chapter06`.

Introducing CartPole-v1

Your task in the CartPole environment is simple: move a cart back and forth along a wire so that a pole pivoting on the cart balances upright. In control theory, this is called the **inverted pendulum** problem, and it is one of several classic control theory problems implemented as reinforcement learning environments in OpenAI Gym.

Here's an illustration of the Gym implementation of the task:

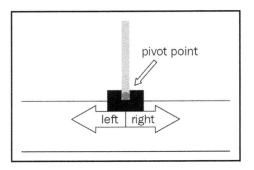

The inverted pendulum as defined in control theory is an underactuated system, meaning it has more degrees of freedom than actuated (controllable) types of movement.

In other words, the position of the cart can be directly controlled, but the movement of the pole cannot. However, the pole can move freely around the joint and the cart can move back and forth. This makes one actuated source of movement and two degrees of freedom.

The inverted pendulum system is unstable but can be controlled, which makes it an interesting problem in mathematics and physics as well as in control system design. Like other underactuated systems, it's often studied in robotics and in other observations of mechanical system stability and control.

Along with CartPole, OpenAI Gym models many interesting and well-known control theory problems such as the mountain car and two-link pendulum as RL environments. We'll explore some of these environments in the final chapter in our discussion of further Q-learning problems to study.

The following shows a CartPole apparatus. We see that the angle between the pole and the vertical line is labeled theta. In the CartPole problem, our job is to minimize theta to keep the pole upright:

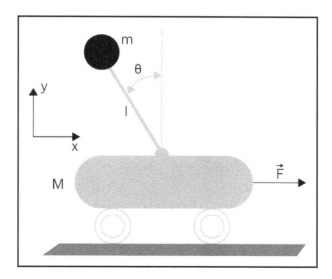

When controlling the CartPole, you'll need to know which direction both the cart and the pole are moving and how fast in order to move the cart in the right direction for the right distance. Observing the problem briefly, we see that moving the cart too far in the direction that the pole is moving will cause the pole to fall. The goal should be to counterbalance the movement of the cart with the movement and angle of the pole.

The two actions you can take are left and right. At each timestep in the task, the agent needs to decide which of these two actions to take.

There are four state (observation) space variables in the CartPole environment:

- Position (x)
- Velocity (x_dot)
- Angle (theta)
- Angular velocity (theta_dot)

All of these variables are continuous, and we receive a new set of observation variables from the environment every timestep. Notice that this is the first time we're working with continuous state space variables in this book.

The CartPole task is solved when the pole stays upright for more than 195 timesteps 100 times in a row. Each episode ends after 200 steps. Note that the pole is considered upright as long as it is less than 15 degrees from vertical.

There are a number of ways to model continuous state spaces when you're enumerating all of the states and explicitly associating actions with those states. One method is to place the states into bins and associate actions with bins of similar states.

Because we're building a DQN and won't be explicitly updating the Q-table ourselves, we won't need to implement this part of the problem, but it's a useful example of how to handle continuous state spaces in general.

Additionally, a deep neural network such as a DQN is able to handle a very large state space, and because Keras provides us with convenient functions to predict values with a network and to fit models to new data, we won't need to implement these operations ourselves.

More about CartPole states and actions

A CartPole state-action-reward diagram might look like the following. Whatever state we're in, we can choose from precisely possible actions (left or right) and can go into one of two other states:

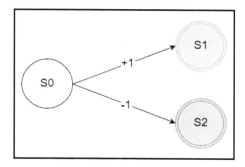

Because the true Q-values of each state depend recursively on the Q-values of later states, as these values backpropagate through the network, the Q-value estimates become more and more accurate. As the multidimensional array of Q-values continues to get updated, the agent's actions become more likely to accurately lead it to winning states.

Getting started with the CartPole task

Let's get an instance of CartPole-v1 running.

We import the necessary package and build the environment with the call to `gym.make()`, as shown in the following code snippet:

```
import gym

env = gym.make('CartPole-v1')
env.reset()

done = False

while not done:
    env.render()
    # Take a random action
    observation, reward, done, info = env.step(env.action_space.sample())
```

We run a loop that renders the environment for a maximum of 1,000 steps. It takes random actions at each timestep using `env.step()`.

Here's the output displaying the CartPole-v1 environment:

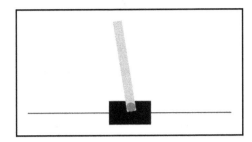

You should see a small window pop up with the CartPole environment displayed.

Because we're taking random actions in our current simulation, we're not taking any of the information about the pole's direction or velocity into account. The pole will quickly fall after a few cycles and the cart will roll off the screen.

In the Taxi environment, taking random actions would eventually lead us to stumble onto a successful pickup. But it's clear that random actions will never get us anywhere in the CartPole task.

Let's briefly consider why this is. Going from one discrete state to another limits our freedom of movement. Eventually, even if after many thousands of moves, we can end up in a success state, because the environment we're working in is ultimately stable. We might run down the clock with too many episodes, but the likelihood that we'll have time to reach a successful drop-off state given thousands of tries is significant.

On the other hand, in an unstable physical system with a continuous state space, with some variables having infinite freedom of movement, the number of potential failure states is so high that it quickly overwhelms the probability that we might accidentally stumble onto a success state. Moreover, success in this task involves sustaining a specific set of states (not allowing the pole to fall more than 15 degrees from vertical) for an extended time.

Clearly, we're going to need to implement a learning algorithm to have any chance of solving the CartPole task. We'll go through how to do this in the next section.

Building a DQN to solve the CartPole problem

In this section, we'll build a deep Q-network using Keras and TensorFlow to solve the CartPole task.

As mentioned in the last chapter, many people incorrectly generalize the term **deep Q-network** to include any Q-learning implementation that uses a neural network. The main distinction between regular neural networks and deep learning is that deep learning structures contain many hierarchical neural network layers constructed into various architectures.

We discussed in the last chapter how to build a single-layer Q-network using TensorFlow at the level of individual layer architecture. Keras allows us to abstract much of the layer-level architecture control that TensorFlow provides. For this reason, we can treat the layer-level mathematical workings of the DQN as a black box at this point.

Refer to the previous chapter for a primer on neural network linear algebra, including dot products and matrix multiplication, to get an understanding of how values propagate through a network.

In general, you won't be making adjustments to the network at the level of the mathematical structure of feedforward and backpropagation functions, so having an overall understanding of deep Q-network functionality will be sufficient for designing RL algorithms.

To get started building the deep Q-network, import the necessary packages:

```
import random
import gym
import numpy as np
from collections import deque
from keras.models import Sequential
from keras.layers import Dense
from keras.optimizers import Adam
```

You should get the message: **Using TensorFlow backend**. If you're familiar with Keras already, you might have also used it with another backend engine such as Theano. Effectively, Keras functions as a wrapper for these backend engines and provides us with many convenient and relatively easy-to-use tools to build deep learning architectures.

Bear in mind that Keras does not depend on either of these specific backend engines to work, just as OpenAI Gym does not make any assumptions about the implementation architecture you use for your RL algorithms.

Next, set up the hyperparameters:

```
gamma = 1
alpha = 0.1
epsilon = 1
epsilon_decay = 0.99
```

What values should we choose for these hyperparameters, and how can we efficiently compare the performance of potential values to each other?

Recall that a grid search is a useful method for comparing the performance of hyperparameter values to each other for optimization purposes. For the purposes of this chapter, we're going to experiment with different values for these hyperparameters and observe in detail how changing the values affects the performance of our model.

Gamma

In this task, we choose a value of 1 for gamma. Recall that gamma determines how much the agent prioritizes current over future rewards. One purpose of gamma is to penalize the agent for taking too long to find a solution.

In the CartPole problem, the agent's goal is to remain active for as long as possible, since in each state the choice is between moving the wrong way and making the pole fall over or moving the right way and keeping it upright.

The only thing that matters to the agent in this task is the next state. For this reason, we want the agent to prioritize staying alive over everything else and not to take future rewards into account at all.

Alpha

The goal of the learning parameter alpha is to smooth out the agent's update curve, protecting it against extreme outliers.

In machine learning terms, a well-chosen alpha value is intended to prevent an RL model from overfitting. In other words, it keeps the model from learning too much from random noise and outliers and from making overly-specific generalizations about the specific data it has already seen.

We choose an alpha parameter for this problem based on the level of generalization we should expect based on the experiences it has had of its environment so far.

Epsilon

Because of the high number of states we'll be working with, we'll start with a high value for epsilon to encourage a high exploration level. When we choose to decay epsilon, we'll do so slowly to allow for as much exploration as possible in the early stages of the task.

Building a DQN class

We're going to put together a basic DQN algorithm that actually progresses through the environment and keeps the CartPole in motion for more than a few steps. We'll build on the performance of this basic algorithm after we see its results, but this will be sufficient to get a solution up and running.

We start by initializing the hyperparameters and the action space:

```
class DQN:

    def __init__(self):
        self.epsilon = epsilon
        self.gamma = gamma
        self.alpha = alpha
        self.action_space = env.action_space.n
```

We're now creating a three-layer sequential network in Keras using `relu` activation functions for the input and hidden layers:

```
        self.model = Sequential()
        self.model.add(Dense(24, input_shape=(observation_space,),
activation="relu"))
        self.model.add(Dense(24, activation="relu"))
        self.model.add(Dense(self.action_space, activation="linear"))
        self.model.compile(loss="mse",
optimizer=Adam(lr=learning_rate_adam))
```

From the last layer, we see that we're using mean squared error as our loss metric and `Adam` as our optimizer. `Adam` is a first-order, gradient-based optimization algorithm that works well on problems with large amounts of data or state spaces.

Choosing actions with epsilon-greedy

The `choose_action` function takes the current state of the agent and chooses an action based on the current values in the Q-table and the value of epsilon (it chooses a random action if a randomly chosen value is less than epsilon). Notice we're using `model.predict()` to retrieve the Q-values. This is a built-in Keras function.

Essentially, the CartPole task is a binary classification problem. The outputs are the two possible actions: left (0) and right (1).

The DQN provides updated estimates for the Q-values through the predict function. When the actual Q-values are provided and the loss backpropagates through the network, the network's weights are updated to reflect this new information about the Q-function.

Recall that this is the basic structure of how neural networks learn and model any system. In this case, the system the DQN is modeling is the agent's actual Q-function. The network will end up with a multidimensional, complex representation of the Q-function mapping states to actions, in which any node can be updated and receive backpropagated values from other nodes in the network:

```
def choose_action(self, state):
    if np.random.rand() < self.exploration_rate:
        return random.randrange(self.action_space)
    q_values = self.model.predict(state)
    return np.argmax(q_values[0])
```

Here, the agent is choosing actions based on the value of epsilon. It chooses either a random action or the action with the current highest Q-value.

We've gone over how to choose the highest Q-valued action using a DQN. In the next section, we'll talk about how to update the Q-values as the agent progresses through the environment and discovers high-valued actions.

Updating the Q-values

The update function modifies the Q-values according to our familiar Bellman equation:

$$NewQ(s, a) = Q(s, a) + \alpha[R(s, a) + \gamma maxQ'(s', a') - Q(s, a)]$$

- **NewQ(s,a)**: New Q value for that state and that action
- **Q(s,a)**: Current Q value
- **α**: Learning Rate
- **R(s,a)**: Reward for taking that action at that state
- **γ**: Discount Rate
- **maxQ'(s',a')**: maximum expected future reward given the new s' and all possible actions at that new state

We use the alpha and gamma values we declared earlier, set the new Q-value for the current state based on the maximum Q-value for the next state, and fit the model to our new state and Q-value:

```
def update(self, state, action, reward, next_state, done):
    q_update = reward
    if not done:
        q_update = self.alpha * (reward + self.gamma *
np.max(self.model.predict(next_state)[0]))
    q_values = self.model.predict(state)
    q_values[0][action] = q_update
    self.model.fit(state, q_values, verbose=0)
```

Again, the basic structure of the Q-function remains the same as in the model-free version. We're still updating the Q-table with the most current Q-value information we have.

The difference here is that the network is providing estimates for the Q-values from its approximation of the agent's Q-function using deep learning operations that are built into the network. We get our approximations for the Q-values with `model.predict()`, and once we get the actual Q-values, we fit our model to them using the `model.fit()` function.

Recall that this difference makes the system policy-based rather than purely value-based, since we are attempting to predict what the Q-values are based on an actual function instead of, as in the case of a value-based system, simply assuming that the agent is always following the best possible policy.

Running the task loop

The full code for this problem is available on GitHub (`https://github.com/PacktPublishing/Hands-On-Q-Learning-with-Python/tree/master/ch6`), but we'll go through key sections of it in this chapter.

In the task loop, we create a DQN and run it over a series of episodes. Each episode lasts a maximum of 200 episodes, or until the task is lost. This happens when the pole falls more than 15 degrees from vertical or the cart moves more than 2.4 units from the center of the screen.

We set `next_state`, reward, done, and info as we did in our previous Q-learning models. (Again, we are not making use of the info variable here.) These variables are set with `env.step(action)` as before.

We initialize the state and fit it as a state vector:

```
def cartpole():
    env = gym.make("CartPole-v1")
    observation_space, action_space = env.observation_space.shape[0],
env.action_space.n
    dqn = DQN(observation_space, action_space)
    run = 0
...
```

The task loop counts the number of steps we've taken in this episode to keep track of how long the CartPole system has stayed alive. The `step` variable keeps count of this as the loop runs, as shown in the following code block:

```
...

        action = dqn.choose_action(state)
        next_state, reward, done, info = env.step(action)
        reward = reward if not done else -reward
        next_state = np.reshape(next_state, [1, observation_space])

        dqn.update(state, action, reward, next_state, done)
        state = next_state
        if done:
            print ("Epoch: " + str(run) + " Score: " + str(step))
            break

if __name__ == "__main__":
    cartpole()
```

We call the update function with the new reward information for the Q-table. When we've finished updating the Q-table, we set the state variable as `next_state` to implement the action that we've taken and continue through the episode.

As the loop runs, the results for each run will be displayed as output. For each episode, we'll see the number of steps the CartPole system stayed active before the pole fell past 15 degrees or the hard limit of 200 timesteps ran out.

A good model should have the CartPole stay active for longer the longer it runs, if it's truly generalizing well from its environment and representing the environment accurately in its state-action function. When we take a look at our own results, we'll see if whether we can make out a pattern of increasing scores per episode and discuss what we can change about the model to improve its performance.

Testing and results

Let's look at the results we see from running this DQN:

```
if __name__ == "__main__":
    cartpole()
```

```
Epoch: 450 Score: 12
Epoch: 451 Score: 24
Epoch: 452 Score: 19
Epoch: 453 Score: 15
Epoch: 454 Score: 16
Epoch: 455 Score: 19
Epoch: 456 Score: 38
Epoch: 457 Score: 18
Epoch: 458 Score: 22
Epoch: 459 Score: 13
Epoch: 460 Score: 19
Epoch: 461 Score: 16
Epoch: 462 Score: 28
Epoch: 463 Score: 10
Epoch: 464 Score: 12
Epoch: 465 Score: 21
Epoch: 466 Score: 14
Epoch: 467 Score: 26
Epoch: 468 Score: 21
Epoch: 469 Score: 22
```

We're definitely making some progress here. We're able to score some points, and the further we go, the higher our score goes, even if the progress is slow. But it still doesn't seem like we're getting consistently closer to solving the task. Our average score isn't climbing high enough to reach the required level.

One issue we might be experiencing is noise in our model. Because there are so many states in our model and so much potential feedback, we might be receiving noisy feedback that's slowing down our model's ability to generalize from the data. Remember that we've chosen a low alpha value to try to cut down on overfitting and too much learning from noise.

What changes can we make now to improve our performance? We can tune the hyperparameters to see if we can set them at more suitable values. We can also try other optimization methods.

To start with, we're going to add in a method called **experience replay** to try to improve our results. Let's talk about what this is and how it works.

Adding in experience replay

Experience replay takes an agent's state-action observations and stores them in a list or table. It then goes through the table periodically and uses some of these observations, chosen at random, to update the Q-table.

Recall that right now our model is updating the Q-table after every action step. We're going to add an experience replay method to our update function that will update our Q-values in randomly selected batches instead.

About experience replay

Why are we choosing to use experience replay? What advantage does it provide over updating the Q-values at every iteration?

Let's first take a look at the loss function for the deep Q-network:

$$Li(\theta i) = E(s, a, r, s)\tilde{}U(D)[(r + \gamma max a' Q(s', a'; \theta - i) - Q(s, a; \theta i))2]$$

Essentially, instead of running an update on the Q-table every time we take an action and getting a max Q-value for the next state, we store the results of each action and then run updates in randomly-chosen batches all at once.

One advantage this provides is the reduction of noise in the model. There are some updates we don't want to incorporate into our Q-function, because they are based on noise, or on a random action that led to results we wouldn't typically see and don't want to generalize about.

Depending on the task, overfitting can be as much a problem in reinforcement learning models as it is in other varieties of machine learning models. We don't want a model being trained on noise, or learning overly specific lessons about a situation that won't apply to other situations it will later find itself in.

Instead, we want it to be able to generalize about its environment in a way that will allow it to make useful predictions about similar future situations.

Recall that a model-free RL solution by definition has **no model**. It cannot generalize about its environment. It cannot make predictions about states it has not yet seen. All it can do is assume the agent is following an optimal policy (Q-learning) or progressively discover the actual policy an agent is following (SARSA). But it has no model of the agent's policy (state-action mapping function) that can be explicitly articulated.

A DQN, on the other hand, builds a model of the agent's policy, making predictions about it at every step, updating these predictions based on its observed loss, and backpropagating them through the network to fit the model to its environment.

As much as possible, we want this model to make use of good data and not to overfit to potential bad data, so that it can make good predictions and generalizations.

This is where experience replay comes in. It does not have the model update the Q-table after every action taken. This makes the model more efficient since it does not have to update as often, and more robust since the batches of updates it receives are randomly chosen and more likely to have outliers flattened out of the distribution.

Implementation

We store the results of each action step in a list called self.memory. When we decide to run the update function, we choose a random sample of action steps stored as memories and update the Q-values of the state-action pairs represented in those memories. The remember function takes the step of storing each memory.

This works very much as if we were updating the Q-values after each action, but in this case we're delaying the updates and not performing them at every step.:

```
def update(self):
        if len(self.memory) < self.batch_size:
            return
        batch = random.sample(self.memory, self.batch_size)
        for state, action, reward, next_state, done in batch:
            q_update = reward
        #predict and update Q-values

            q_values = self.model.predict(state)
            ...
```

This helps us cut down on noise, because randomly sampling the memory space makes it less likely we'll choose outlier action steps to update from. In this way our distribution of actions is smoothed out.

Experience replay results

We obtain the results of running our new experience replay function. The following are globally the results we obtained from running the task in our implementation:

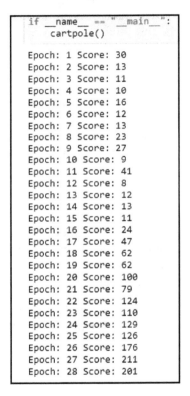

```
if __name__ == "__main__":
    cartpole()

Epoch: 1 Score: 30
Epoch: 2 Score: 13
Epoch: 3 Score: 11
Epoch: 4 Score: 10
Epoch: 5 Score: 16
Epoch: 6 Score: 12
Epoch: 7 Score: 13
Epoch: 8 Score: 23
Epoch: 9 Score: 27
Epoch: 10 Score: 9
Epoch: 11 Score: 41
Epoch: 12 Score: 8
Epoch: 13 Score: 12
Epoch: 14 Score: 13
Epoch: 15 Score: 11
Epoch: 16 Score: 24
Epoch: 17 Score: 47
Epoch: 18 Score: 62
Epoch: 19 Score: 62
Epoch: 20 Score: 100
Epoch: 21 Score: 79
Epoch: 22 Score: 124
Epoch: 23 Score: 110
Epoch: 24 Score: 129
Epoch: 25 Score: 126
Epoch: 26 Score: 176
Epoch: 27 Score: 211
Epoch: 28 Score: 201
```

We can clearly see that the agent is learning much rapidly with experience replay and that its achievement curve is much steeper. It quickly starts to average scores of 195 or higher continuously, allowing it to complete the task successfully.

Building further on DQNs

There are several improvements and additions to deep Q-networks that are worth exploring broadly here. We won't be working with these algorithms directly in this chapter, but this is a good starting point for finding ways to improve the performance of the DQNs you've built so far.

Calculating DQN loss

Calculating the prediction loss in a DQN (also called the **TD** or **Temporal Difference** error) is a matter of finding the difference between the true Q-value of a state-action pair and the value estimated by the network. We then backpropagate the loss to the earlier nodes in the network to update their weights.

The issue we run into is that **we don't actually know the true Q-value of a state**. We are estimating it using some version of the following Bellman equation:

$$Q(s, a) = r(s, a) + \gamma max a Q(s', a)$$

- **Q(s,a)**: Q target
- **r(s,a)**: Reward of taking that action at that state
- **γmax$_a$Q(s´,a)**: Discounted max q value among all possible actions from next state

Until our running tabulation of the true Q-values of the environment converges, we are trying to predict a set of targets that is itself an estimate of the actual Q-function. The same set of weights is being applied to both the target and the predicted values when calculating the loss:

$$\triangle w = \alpha[(R + \gamma max_a \hat{Q}(s', a, w)) - \hat{Q}(s, a, w)]\nabla_w \hat{Q}(s, a, w)$$

Because we are using the same network weights to estimate both the current Q-value and the target we're predicting (the actual Q-value), there is a high correlation between the two sets of estimates. This leads to high oscillation—meaning poor performance – in the training process.

The overall effect is that the network is chasing a target that is moving as it tries to estimate it. We'll go over a few solutions and workarounds to this problem here.

Fixed Q-targets

The fixed Q-targets solution was introduced by the DeepMind team. Using two DQNs instead of one, this method keeps the target values of one network (called the **target network**) fixed and periodically updates the network weights.

Here's a sample implementation of a target network in Keras:

```
class DQN:
    def __init__(self, state_size, action_size):
        self.model = self._build_model()
        self.target_model = self._build_model()
        self.update_target_model()
    def update_target_model(self):
        self.target_model.set_weights(self.model.get_weights())
```

For most of the training process, the weights in the target network are fixed, taking away the problem of trying to predict a moving target.

Double-deep Q-networks

The problem of **maximization bias** occurs when a network consistently overestimates the Q-values leading to the states it might end up in as a result of each potential action. This happens often at the beginning of training, where the DQN is still working with very noisy estimates of Q-values.

One alternative implementation of a DQN called a **double-deep Q-network** splits the process of choosing actions using two networks. One network is responsible for choosing the next action, which as usual will be the action with the highest Q-value. The other network, called the target network, carries out the process of evaluating and updating the Q-value of taking that action.

Decoupling these two functions cuts down on maximization bias and leads to faster and more effective training by effectively solving the moving target problem.

Dueling deep Q-networks

The Q-value of a state can be decomposed to two values:

- *V(s)*: The value of currently being in state *s*
- *A(s, a)*: The advantage of taking action *a* from state *s* over all the other actions the agent could take from state *s*

$$Q(s,a) = A(s,a) + V(s)$$

Dueling deep Q-networks separate out the estimators of these two values, using a different DQN to calculate each of the values for *V(s)* and *A(s, a)*. They then combine the two values into an overall Q-value using an aggregating layer.

Here's a sample network architecture to accomplish this:

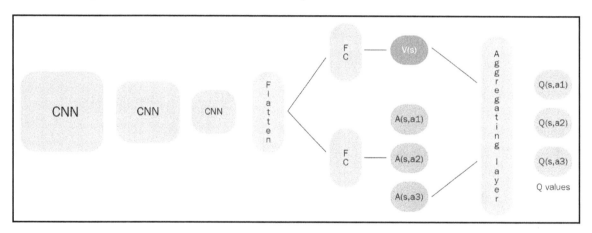

One positive effect of separating out these two calculations is that we no longer need to consider the effect of actions that could be taken from a state that does not affect the environment and can be ignored, freeing up computing time for evaluating actions that are potentially valuable.

The learning agent can also learn which states are inherently not valuable and should be avoided in any case without having to calculate the value of each action from that state.

Summary

We've designed and built our first deep Q-network to solve the CartPole problem. Deep Q-networks handle the problem of what happens when a state space in an optimization task gets too large to handle with a simple lookup table function.

DQNs are able to model a state space and the Q-function of an agent, allowing the agent to generalize about the environment and predict the values of states it has not yet seen. Keras provides many useful functionalities that let us design and build powerful DQN architectures relatively quickly and easily.

In the next chapter, we'll dive deeper into a particularly interesting problem in RL called the **multi-armed bandit problem (MABP)**, its relevance to scientific research, and the types of problems that are well-suited to this problem-solving framework.

Questions

1. What is the difference between using Keras as a wrapper for TensorFlow and using TensorFlow by itself?
2. What kind of prediction problem is CartPole? What type of target is being predicted?
3. What advantage does binning the state space provide?
4. Give a 2–3 sentence explaining how experience replay works.
5. Explain the moving target problem in estimating Q-values.
6. Explain what maximization bias is.
7. When does maximization bias tend to happen?
8. What advantage do dueling DQNs provide over regular DQNs?

Further reading

- Dueling network architectures for deep reinforcement learning: `https://arxiv.org/abs/1511.06581`
- DeepMind DQN: `https://deepmind.com/research/dqn/`
- Episodic memory deep Q-networks: `https://www.ijcai.org/proceedings/2018/0337.pdf`

3
Section 3: Advanced Q-Learning Challenges with Keras, TensorFlow, and OpenAI Gym

The reader will be introduced to more advanced Q-learning problems and will get suggestions on how to take an RL approach to real-world problems. They will become familiar with research in Q-learning and the current problems practitioners are working on solving. They will leave this section with a sense of what is coming up next in RL and how they can apply their skills to those problems moving forward.

The following chapters are included in this section:

- Chapter 7, *Decoupling Exploration and Exploitation in Multi-Armed Bandits*
- Chapter 8, *Further Q-Learning Research and Future Projects*

7
Decoupling Exploration and Exploitation in Multi-Armed Bandits

In this chapter, we will dive deeper into the topic of multi-armed bandits. We touched on the basics of how they work in Chapter 1, *Brushing Up on Reinforcement Learning Concepts*, and we'll go over some of the conclusions we reached there. We'll extend our knowledge of the exploration-versus-exploitation process that we learned from our study of Q-learning and apply it to other optimization problems using Q-values and exploration-based strategies.

We will do the following in this chapter:

- Understand a simple bandit problem in greater detail
- Learn the effect of adding a state to the description of the bandit's environment
- Become familiar with more advanced bandit-type research problems in various fields
- Understand the benefits of bandit-type implementations in experimental trials using A/B testing
- Discuss a simple solution to an ad-click problem in Python

Technical requirements

You will need the following packages installed to complete the exercises in this chapter:

- Python 3.5+
- NumPy
- Pandas (for working with flat dataframes)

We will not be using the OpenAI Gym package in this chapter, but it will be helpful to be familiar with it and the projects we've worked through using the introductory Gym environments at this point. If you haven't completed the projects in the previous chapters, we recommend you do so before diving into this chapter.

We strongly encourage you to familiarize yourself with the official OpenAI Gym documentation for the Taxi-v2 environment as well as the other environments we will be working with in this book. You will find a great deal of useful information on these environments and how to access the information and functionality you need from them. You can find the documentation here: `https://gym.openai.com/docs/`.

The code for the exercises in this chapter can be found here: `https://github.com/PacktPublishing/Hands-On-Q-Learning-with-Python/tree/master/Chapter07`.

Probability distributions and ongoing knowledge

In a reinforcement learning task, our goal is to take our increasing knowledge of a problem and use it to our advantage. We are not simply trying to gain the clearest possible picture of a problem; we are trying to benefit from the knowledge we currently have and not get distracted by potentially interesting alternative paths that might not be to our advantage to follow, and that in fact may harm us.

Let's briefly discuss what our ongoing investigation of a probability distribution looks like:

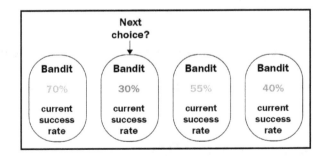

The preceding diagram shows what our current success rate might look like at any particular time in a bandit problem for all of the arms available to us. If we had conducted 1,000 trials already, for example, we might have discovered these success rates for each arm. On any particular trial, we would use that knowledge to decide which arm to pull next.

Once we've done enough trials, our observations start to converge and the probabilities of success we observe vary less than they did at the beginning of our experimentation. When this happens, we can feel confident that we're getting closer to the true probability distribution.

Iterative probability distributions

We can think of a probability distribution of the likelihood of an event as the distribution we would find if we could conduct infinite trials of the problem and tabulate all the outcomes we saw.

Some commonly-known probability distributions are shown in the following figure. You're probably familiar with the normal (Gaussian) distribution, which is commonly used to model populations in the natural and social sciences and used in many other contexts:

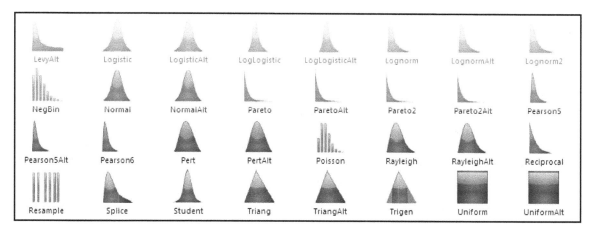

Clearly, in a real-world problem we cannot conduct infinite trials of an experiment. We can conduct a specific number of trials: for example, 100 trials, 1,000 trials, or 100 million trials. Our knowledge of the problem changes progressively as we conduct these trials. As we make more observations, we incorporate them into our existing likelihood counts.

The more trials we conduct, the closer we will come to the true probability distribution of the problem. But our knowledge of the true probability distribution will get better and better in parallel. This will get us close enough to the true distribution to be able to make good decisions based on our knowledge of it.

As we iterate through trials or episodes, we can chart our changing probability distribution for each arm and detect the overall likelihood of success for each one.

The preceding experiment uses the epsilon-greedy algorithm, which uses an epsilon value of 10% (it initiates 10% random actions and 90% optimal Q-valued actions). We'll go through a comparison of the epsilon-greedy strategy with other potential strategies in the next section.

It's also not sufficient in most real-world optimization problems to wait until we have some arbitrary amount of knowledge about a problem to be able to make real-time decisions about it. We want to be able to *learn as we go* and to take advantage of the knowledge we have now, even with the awareness that our knowledge and the decisions we make will change in the future.

Specifically, let's say that arm 1 or arm 2 of a bandit yields higher rewards in our early trials. We would want to take advantage of that knowledge now even knowing that other arms might get us higher rewards in the future.

This is the balance we try to strike with the exploration-versus-exploitation dynamic. We quantify the amount of exploration we want to do with our epsilon factor, and we adjust it as our number of trials increases and our recorded probability distribution changes.

Revisiting a simple bandit problem

The simplest kind of **Multi-Armed Bandit Problem** (**MABP**) is a two-armed bandit. At each iteration, we have a choice of one of two arms to pull, as well as our current knowledge of the payout probability of each arm. We'll go through a demonstration of a two-armed bandit iteration in this section.

As we progress through our investigation, we want to look at our existing knowledge of the probability distribution of the payout for each arm. This will help us determine our betting strategy.

When we first start to investigate the frequency of an unknown event, we start with no information on the likelihood of that event occurring. It's useful to think of the probability distribution we develop over time as our own level of knowledge about that event, and conversely our own ignorance about it.

In other words, we only have the information we have now about any particular bandit. We are not aware of its true probability distribution. As we learn more about it, we might change our perception of what outcomes we're likely to see, and consequently change the decisions we make. The more investigation we do on the likelihood of an event occurring, the closer we come to knowing its true probability distribution.

A sample two-armed bandit iteration

For each iteration of the MABP task, we have two arms we can potentially pull. When we first start, we have no knowledge of how often either arm will pay out. Our overall goal is to maximize our long-term payout. We start out in an exploration phase and pull each arm multiple times to see how often it pays out.

For example, take the following Bernoulli (binary) bandit, where the payout is either 0 or 1:

Trial	Arm	Reward
1	1	0
2	2	1
3	1	1
4	2	0
5	1	1
6	2	0
7	1	1
8	2	1
9	1	1
10	2	1

Effectively, this is pure exploration. We are simply switching between arms here, not yet looking at the results we are getting in deciding which arm to pull next. We are not using any other strategy yet, and we are not taking advantage of the results we have gotten, because we are just starting out in the exploration process.

Let's look at our probability distribution so far. By the end of 9 trials, we have the following results:

- **Arm 1**: 5 pulls, 4 wins, 80% success
- **Arm 2**: 5 pulls, 3 wins, 60% success

Based on these results, which is the better arm to pull at this point? If we had to choose one arm and only pull that one, which would it be?

One answer is that we just don't know enough about the problem yet. We don't have a large enough number of trials to have a reliable idea of what the true probability distribution is for each arm.

Ideally, if we continued to explore, we would get a larger sample size of observations, and we would be in a better place to make a decision.

Another answer is that we should decide now what strategy we want to follow, without having full knowledge of whether it is the best possible strategy, and adapt our responses to the feedback we get over time.

This is the basis of exploration versus exploitation. We don't want to wait until we have full knowledge of the problem to start taking advantage of the knowledge we already have.

The flipside of this is that we don't want to find a good strategy and keep exploiting it at the expense of finding potentially better strategies. This can lead to getting stuck on local maxima, a problem we've discussed in previous chapters.

Multi-armed bandit strategy overview

Let's go through a brief comparison of some popular action selection strategies. We'll focus on a few in particular:

- Greedy strategy
- Epsilon-greedy strategy
- Upper confidence bound

Outside the AI space, reinforcement learning is often referred to as dynamic programming. Upper confidence bound is a strategy often used in the dynamic programming space in fields such as economics. It is based on the principle of optimism in the face of uncertainty and places a high priority on exploration.

Using upper confidence bound, we assume we are better off exploring our environment as much as we can and presuming that paths we have not seen will lead to high rewards. We'll see how this works in the following strategy selection sections.

Greedy strategy

The greedy strategy tells us we should always pick the highest-valued action we have seen so far, without doing any exploration at all. As we've discussed, this can lead to getting stuck on a local maximum, or an action that currently has a higher Q-value than the other actions we could take from that state.

Using the greedy strategy, we would continue to follow that local maximum reward path even though there might be other potential actions we could take that would have higher Q-values once we progressed through those reward gradients. For that reason, we see that the greedy strategy would allow us to get stuck on a suboptimal action path forever, with no option for exploring alternatives.

Epsilon-greedy strategy

By introducing an exploratory epsilon factor, we immediately improve on the simple greedy strategy by guaranteeing that at least some exploration will take place and we won't get stuck pulling the same currently high-valued arms over and over.

One way to compare strategies is by looking at their total reward, meaning the reward we collect over the course of all of the trial runs through the testing cycle.

We see the results of running a random sampler action-selection method in the following screenshot. Each arm gets chosen roughly the same number of times, no matter the results it gets:

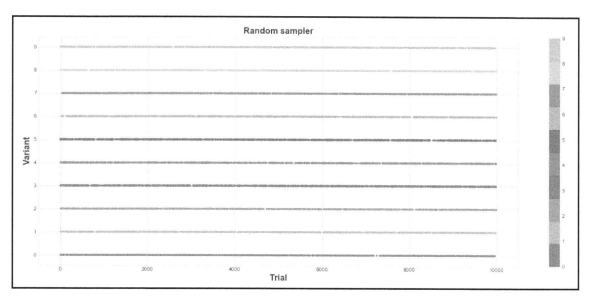

The preceding screenshot shows how often a 10-armed bandit learner chooses an optimal arm using a random strategy. When the epsilon-greedy bandit determines that arm number 5, for example, is a high-reward arm, it chooses to pull that arm more often, until it's pulling that arm almost all the time.

In this case, arm 5 is not the optimal arm, but it's close to the optimal arm, and epsilon-greedy has allowed us to find it where the random strategy wouldn't have. A more selective strategy improves on a random or simple greedy strategy by keeping track of the results so far and focusing its efforts on high-yield areas of the environment.

Upper confidence bound

Upper confidence bound is another action selection approach we can take.

The goal of upper confidence bound is to make sure we don't continue to take random actions we've already taken and that have given us poor results. It prioritizes action spaces with high uncertainty (spaces we haven't explored yet at all get priority over spaces we have explored). Essentially, we are putting an upper limit on the **utility** (value) of a potential action.

In a Bayesian UCB strategy, we estimate a prior probability distribution for the reward (such as Gaussian). In other strategies we don't assume any prior distributions and use other types of estimate instead (such as Hoeffding's inequality).

The following distributions are three Gaussian probability distributions with different mean and standard distribution values:

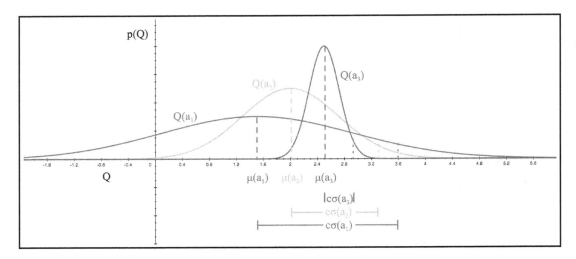

We adjust the hyperparameter **c** to change the shape of the distribution curve. (Recall that a hyperparameter is a parameter value that we choose ourselves and is not determined within the problem.)

Bandit regret

The overall loss we incur due to picking non-optimal arms throughout our series of trials is called **regret**. We treat regret as a variable we want to minimize, in the vein of an error term when evaluating the performance of a machine learning model.

We calculate regret as the difference between the rewards we would expect an optimal strategy to collect and the actual rewards we have collected so far. In economics terms, regret is a measure of lost utility.

 Utility is a term taken from economics and refers in reinforcement learning problems to the value given by the Q-function.

Utility functions and optimal decisions

It's helpful to think of reinforcement learning agents, and all optimizing agents, as operating under the constraint of a *utility function*. In the case of our Q-learning agents, the utility functions they're working with are what we call the *policies* they're following. We can think of the Q-value of an action as its utility.

A utility in real-life terms is a reward, such as money, that either can or can't be easily quantified. It is the reward an agent is pursuing and gauging its actions and decisions against. For real-world learning agents such as human beings, utility functions are obviously complex and involve many different kinds of motivations and drivers that interact with each other in ways that are difficult to quantify.

Regardless, when we want to predict the behavior of an agent, or when we want to implement an agent that will pursue a particular goal, a utility function is a straightforward and consistent model to use and to try to approximate. We might never know an agent's true utility function, and we may never know the actual optimal action to take in a situation depending on the problem, but if we're able to learn from our past actions and change our future actions based on what we learned, we can get as close as possible to it.

Contextual bandits and state diagrams

Multi-armed bandits, like other reinforcement learning agents, benefit from being able to learn from long-term feedback. One way to implement this is to introduce states into the multi-armed bandit model:

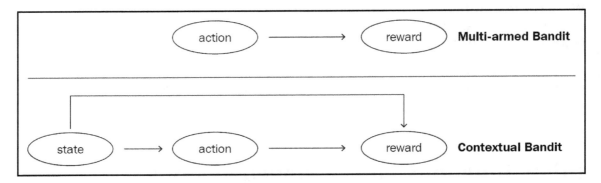

What advantage does being able to differentiate states from each other give to the bandit?

If we're deciding which advertisements to show to an app user, for example, it might be helpful to have some consistent outside knowledge about that user and to take that knowledge into account. With no state information, all we would know is how successful that advertisement was for overall users. With state information, the model would have access to factors such as the user's age, gender, or income, and be able to make more targeted predictions based on that knowledge.

We also wouldn't have to limit our model to just demographic information about users. If we had access to information about user behavior, such as previous page views or advertisement clicks, we could make even more targeted predictions based on that information.

For example, we might know that 10% of the users we've surveyed will click on a particular advertisement, but we might also know that 20% of the women we've surveyed will click on that ad, or that 5% of college students will click on it. If our model takes into account whether a user is a woman or a college student, it can make a better prediction about whether they will click on that advertisement or not.

The simple bandit examples we'll be working with in Python won't incorporate states, but it's an avenue of research worth exploring as you get further into reinforcement learning and its applications.

Thompson sampling and the Bayesian control rule

We'll go over the concepts of Thompson sampling and Bayesian control problems at a high level, but they are well worth exploring further as an extension of the topics covered in this book.

Thompson sampling

Essentially, Thompson sampling has us believing what the prior probability distribution is and updating it every time we get new information about the environment. Eventually, our updated belief will coincide with the true probability distribution. This approach is fundamentally Bayesian. This is because it treats the probability distribution as our current lack of knowledge about the environment and updates it according to the new information we get.

In Thompson sampling, we are working with a contextual (state-based) bandit framework. The agent receives information about its state, the actions available to it, and the current Q-values of those actions.

We start with a prior likelihood distribution on each action A based on our current knowledge of it. Effectively, the Thompson sampling model chooses actions according to its belief that taking those actions will maximize the expected reward for each iteration:

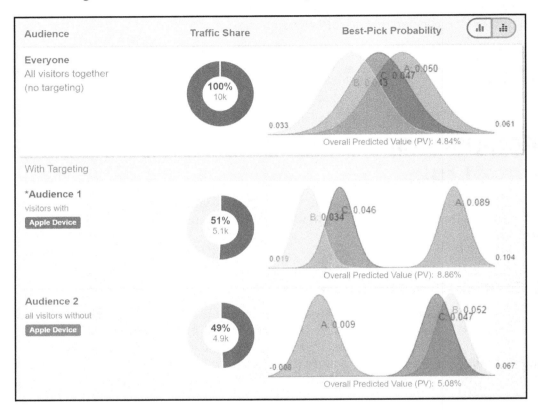

In the preceding example, we separate out the visitors to a site by targeting them based on whether they are using an Apple device or not. Option A (which might be an advertisement) performs better on users with Apple devices, but much worse on users without Apple devices.

If we had not separated out the distributions for those two groups, we would have only known that A was performing slightly better than B and C overall, and would have chosen it every time, whereas the optimal choice would be to select A for users with Apple devices and not to select it for users without Apple devices.

Thompson sampling was first described in 1933 by the philosopher William R. Thompson, but it has been rediscovered and reformulated multiple times by AI researchers. We'll discuss more general formulations of the process in the next section.

Bayesian control rule

The Bayesian control rule is a generalization of the Thompson sampling process that has the agent develop general rules about causal relationships in the environment. Briefly, as it interacts with the environment, it codifies these causal relationships and adopts a behavior that maximizes its own utility with respect to the environment.

Here is a brief primer on Bayes' rule and priors: in probability terms, a *prior distribution* is our current estimate of what the likelihood of an event is, and a posterior distribution is our estimate of the likelihood of that event once we run a trial on it and get additional information about it.

This is the Bayesian approach to assigning probability distributions to unknown future events:

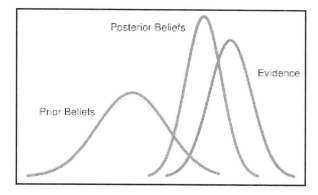

The preceding figure is a general depiction of how a prior distribution changes after the addition of evidence and observations. The new distribution, our **Posterior Beliefs** about the distribution, is shown in the middle.

In the case of potential customers of an online advertisement, we might be given a large potential sample of users of an app, such as 10,000 users, and told that 10% of these users will click on the app. (The numbers we're using are simplified for the purpose of this example.)

If this is all the information we are given about customers, then for any potential customer we will assume that they have a 10% chance of clicking on the app. We make decisions accordingly for each customer.

If we are then told when a customer owns an Apple device, and that 20% of Apple users are likely to click on the ad, then we can shift our likelihood estimate of that particular customer's clicking on the advertisement from 10% to 20%.

We are *updating our beliefs* about that customer (adjusting the probability estimate for the demographic they belong to).

In other words, when we first assumed they had a 10% chance of clicking on the ad, we would have shown them that advertisement accordingly, but now that we know they are an Apple device user and are more likely to click the ad, we can show it to them more often. This is the process of updating our beliefs based on new information we are given.

The process of applying Thompson sampling or the Bayesian control rule to a set of data consists of sampling that data, running RL models over that data, and updating the probability assumptions of the model based on it. The sampler selects from the data based on a specified set of variants, such as user demographics in the previous example.

Let's discuss how to solve a multi-armed bandit problem using a simulated set of ad-click data. We'll provide the code you'll need to run the example in the GitHub repository for the chapter.

Solving a multi-armed bandit problem in Python – user advertisement clicks

In this section we'll be solving a multi-armed bandit problem using a simulated set of ad-click data. We'll generate a set of clicks for 5 different advertisements. Each ad will either be clicked or not clicked when it is shown to a user. Our goal is to determine which ad to show next based on how each ad is performing at any given point in the simulation.

We start with a baseline loop that chooses a random advertisement from the selection each time. This model does not learn from its actions and always chooses a random action. If the user clicks on the ad, we get a reward of 1; if not, we get a reward of 0.

We import the necessary packages and generate a data frame of simulated data using random numbers. We will specify a distribution of 90% zero values and 10% 1 values for this example:

```
import numpy as np
import pandas as pd
import matplotlib.pyplot as plt
import random
```

```
df = pd.DataFrame(np.random.choice(np.arange(0, 2), p=[0.9,
0.1],size=(10000, 5)), columns=list('ABCDE'))
```

Note that, because the data is simulated, we'll be regenerating it each time we run the example.

Here's a screenshot of the dataframe we generated:

In [28]:	**df**					
Out[28]:						
		A	**B**	**C**	**D**	**E**
	0	0	0	0	0	0
	1	0	0	0	0	0
	2	0	0	0	0	0
	3	0	0	0	0	0
	4	0	0	0	0	0
	5	0	1	0	0	1
	6	0	0	0	0	0
	7	0	0	0	0	0
	8	0	1	0	0	0
	9	0	0	0	0	0
	10	1	0	0	0	0
	11	0	0	0	0	0
	12	0	0	0	0	0

```
total_views = 10000
num_ads = 5
ad_list = []
total = 0

for view in range(total_views):
    ad = random.randrange(num_ads)
    ad_list.append(ad)
    reward = df.values[view, ad]
    total = total + reward
```

Here, we have run the `value_counts()` function on the advertisement list. We have a list of ads we've shown so far, and the total rewards that we collected from showing each ad.

We see that advertisement **0** is the best-performing ad, and that advertisement **1** is the worst-performing. In other examples, we could make the distribution of clicks less uniform, so that the variation in click results between each advertisement a higher. This would bring us closer to a real-life distribution, where some ads perform significantly better than others:

```
In [33]:  pd.Series(ad_list).value_counts(normalize=True)

Out[33]:  0    0.2057
          2    0.2006
          3    0.2000
          4    0.1991
          1    0.1946
          dtype: float64
```

Once again, we treat the randomly acting agent as our baseline model. The agent is not learning anything from its actions, so it chooses each arm with about equal frequency. We'd like to be able to improve on this result using a more selective algorithm.

Epsilon-greedy selection

Our technique in implementing an epsilon-greedy selection is by now a familiar process:

- Choose an epsilon value
- Select a random value; if it is lower than epsilon, take a random action, and if it's higher, take the highest Q-valued action

We've begun the process of implementing an epsilon-greedy algorithm:

```
for view in range(total_views):
    if random.random() < epsilon
    #exploration option: choose a random action

        ad = random.randrange(num_ads)
    else:

        #choose the best-performing ad so far
    ...

    reward = df.values[view, ad]
    total = total + reward
```

In the generalized bandit example, epsilon-greedy uses an epsilon value to decide whether to choose the current **Best arm** (exploit) or a random arm (explore). The following chart demonstrates epsilon-greedy's process for choosing an arm:

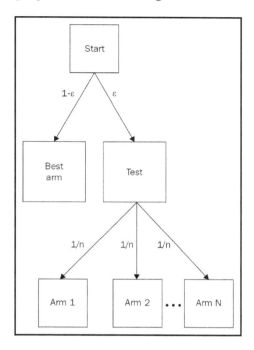

If the value of a random number we choose is greater than epsilon, we choose the current highest-valued arm. If it is less than epsilon, we choose a random arm (this is the **Test** bubble) and go into the exploration phase.

As we progress through testing, epsilon decays after each cycle. In this case, we've chosen a static value for epsilon, but there are many ways we can adapt our choice to the problem and the information we have available.

Multi-armed bandits in experimental design

The merits of multi-armed bandit testing against A/B testing are quickly becoming prominent in the AI research space with the growing availability of experimental data and the ability of researchers to quickly and easily run simultaneous and repeated trials and construct models against that data.

You might be familiar with A/B testing as a scientific process that tests a control population against a variant and compares the results of some process on the two groups, for example, an experimental medical drug that researchers are interested in measuring varying outcomes for.

Outside research sciences and fields such as healthcare, A/B testing is becoming increasingly popular with marketers in the online advertising space. In the next section we will fully explore how the process works.

Essentially, a multi-armed bandit approach to an experimental setup incorporates a feedback loop into an A/B testing process. A/B testing compares two ads against each other using two static testing groups, while multi-armed bandit testing works over multiple trials and chooses ads to show based on the current performance of the ads it has already observed.

How can multi-armed bandits be used to improve on A/B testing, and will they actually perform better? There is a lot of excitement around the idea of new ways of choosing hypotheses, sample sizes, and statistical significance levels in the AI community, and it's worth being familiar with these arguments and continuing to research them. We'll give a brief overview here.

Multi-armed bandit testing is a more dynamic process and allows a recommendation system to learn from its previous experiences with a particular ad. When we are only interested in running a few tests over a short period of time and are monitoring their results closely, A/B testing will often suit our purposes just fine.

However, when we are running more rounds of testing and when we need to iterate on the actions we take as well as the results we observe, multi-armed bandit testing allows us to automate the process and take advantage of our findings faster.

The testing process

In a typical instance of A/B testing, a marketer separates a group of users randomly into two groups and sends them each a version of an advertisement. The advertisement that gets the most clicks or conversions, depending on the performance metric used, is used the next time instead of the one that performed less well:

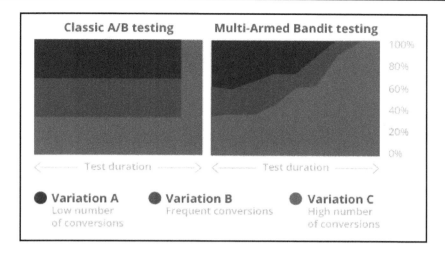

The preceding figure illustrates a typical comparison of three variations on an advertisement (**A**, **B**, and **C**). We can consider classic A/B testing to be using pure exploration with zero exploitation. We run some fixed number of trials, testing each option equally, and the one that performs best is the one that we use. Actually using the variation that performed best can be considered our exploitation phase.

In the multi-armed bandit variation, all three versions are being considered at the same time, and we are using a mix of exploration and exploitation, so we end up using the current highest-performing variation (version C) more often.

There is no clear shift between phases of training and actual implementation (*learning versus earning*). We are using the information we have as we go through the process to maximize our outcomes even as we learn more about the environment, and our conclusions about it end up changing.

Bandits with knapsacks – more multi-armed bandit applications

One interesting variation on the multi-armed bandit problem is bandits with knapsacks. This formulation of the problem was introduced in 2013 and adds in an aspect of resource consumption by the learning agent. The agent has until its resources run out to maximize its reward output.

The bandits with knapsacks formulation is especially useful in economics in framing concepts such as dynamic pricing, where a seller might offer different prices to a customer based on what each customer would be likely to pay. It has many other applications in large-scale finance problems.

Summary

We've gone over multi-armed bandit problems in detail and discussed practical ways in which they can be applied to real-world problems such as advertising and product testing. We've introduced different approaches to solving the problem and suggested opportunities for further research into each of these approaches.

This is only an introduction to the multi-armed bandit problem space, which is well worth researching further and has many exciting applications to explore.

In the next chapter, we'll explore further the types of problems we can solve using our knowledge of Q-learning, including the additional environments offered by OpenAI Gym. We'll leave you with ideas for future projects to develop your skills as a RL practitioner and researcher and you'll be familiar with many of the domains in which you can practice your skills.

Questions

1. What is the true probability distribution of an event? How can we discover what this distribution is?
2. Why is it more useful to conduct 1,000 trials of an experiment than 10 trials? Give a general explanation in 2–3 sentences.
3. Explain the importance of having a large enough sample size when conducting an experiment.
4. Explain what Thompson sampling is in 2–3 sentences.
5. Explain how the Bayesian control rule relates to Thompson sampling.
6. Briefly explain the difference between A/B testing and MAB testing.
7. Why are user ad-clicks a useful demonstration of this type of testing methodology? What might another good example problem be?

Further reading

- *From Ads to Interventions: Contextual Bandits in Mobile Health*: `https://ambujtewari.github.io/research/tewari17ads.pdf`
- *Best Arm Identification in Multi-Armed Bandits*: `http://sbubeck.com/COLT10_ABM.pdf`
- *Episodic Multi-armed Bandits*: `https://arxiv.org/pdf/1508.00641.pdf`
- *A Practical Method for Solving Contextual Bandit Problems Using Decision Trees*: `http://auai.org/uai2017/proceedings/papers/171.pdf`

Further Q-Learning Research and Future Projects

8

We'll wrap up this exploration of Q-learning by discussing some future projects you can work on to build your skills as a **reinforcement learning** (**RL**) researcher and practitioner. We'll also discuss some other publications and sources of information you might find interesting and helpful as you continue your work in this discipline.

In the course of this chapter, we'll be finding additional tools and frameworks we can use with OpenAI Gym, as well as more environments to work with. Gym has a wealth of environments you can use to build your RL algorithm design skills. In addition, it gives you the ability to create your own environments for others to use.

We'll also become familiar with interesting and difficult problems that the RL community is working on, with examples such as recommendation systems. We'll also get into understanding why exploration versus exploitation-type design can sometimes be a better method than A/B testing in scientific trials.

The following topics will be covered briefly in this chapter:

- Google's DeepMind and the future of Q-learning
- OpenAI Gym and RL research
- More OpenAI Gym environments
- Contextual bandits and probability distributions

Google's DeepMind and the future of Q-learning

DeepMind Technologies is an artificial intelligence research firm established in 2010 and is currently a subsidiary of Alphabet Inc., the parent company of Google.

One of DeepMind's most famous successes is AlphaGo, the RL Go-playing machine that beat the current world champion and became the subject of a documentary. Another DeepMind RL agent, AlphaZero, taught itself to play and win not only Go, but also chess and shogi.

All of these machines, like the algorithms we've designed, used RL algorithms with deep learning architectures and taught themselves to play by starting with trial and error, then learning to model the games they were playing as state-action functions.

In December 2013, the DeepMind team developed and introduced deep Q-learning as an algorithm for solving optimization problems with better-than-human success. The company was acquired by Google for $500 million in 2014.

 The graph in the following website shows the performance of DeepMind's AlphaStar on StarCraft II: https://healthytopic.org/deepmind-ai-challenges-pro-starcraft-ii-players-wins-almost-every-match-extremetech/

Today, deep Q-learning and other reinforcement learning algorithms are rapidly changing many fields and delivering on the promise of better-than-human artificial intelligence. DeepMind itself has developed a neural Turing machine, a network that can access an external memory like a conventional Turing machine and is capable of inferring algorithms from inputs and outputs alone.

In addition to the rest of its cutting-edge research, many DeepMind projects involve RL tasks very similar to the ones we've already researched and worked on throughout this book, especially involving continuous control problems and robot locomotion.

We'll be diving into more of the OpenAI Gym implementations of these environments later in the chapter, and it's worth researching some of the creative solutions the DeepMind team, as well as other research laboratories, have developed using powerful RL algorithms.

OpenAI Gym and RL research

As we discussed in the first chapter, OpenAI Gym is an attempt to standardize reinforcement learning research and development and to compare RL models to each other for the purposes of developing baseline research frameworks.

The following screenshot is a still from the Neon Race Car environment with OpenAI Gym and Universe:

As RL researchers, we want to be able to develop benchmarks and widely-used, well-known training and testing datasets like the ones available for supervised learning, such as ImageNet for image recognition, the familiar iris dataset from the UCI Machine Learning Repository, or the MNIST handwritten digit dataset.

The RL analogue for a widely-used labeled training dataset is a standardized set of environments such as the one that Gym provides. A standardized set of environments lets us compare the work of different researchers, working in different institutions, writing different papers, operating under different research methodologies, and incorporating different assumptions to each other. It lets us evaluate their performance on a level playing field.

Without a standardized set of environments, even small differences in an RL implementation, such as the reward structure or state space enumeration, can change the difficulty level of the task and shift the focus away from the actual mechanics of the RL algorithm, making it much more difficult to compare performance across model implementations.

The standardization of RL research practice with Gym

As the field's designated standardized repository of environments, Gym models a number of classic control theory problems that we'll discuss in the next section. It also models some supervised learning problems that have structured or sequential outputs, such as in natural language processing.

In working with Gym, we'll find problems specific to robotics research, such as motion control as well as classic control theory problems and familiar arcade games. Perhaps most interestingly, we'll find environments intended to mimic algorithmic processes, such as copying characters to a tape and learning to add numbers.

Tracking your scores with the Gym leaderboard

For the purposes of comparing your model performance to that of other researchers, the OpenAI Gym leaderboard allows you to add your scores on Gym tasks to a wiki and submit links to your code and to videos and write-ups of your performance. Each task has its own score sheet, and anyone can edit the wiki to include their own scores.

 The Gym leaderboard can be found at `https://github.com/openai/gym/wiki/Leaderboard`.

The wiki also includes detailed descriptions of each environment that anyone can edit. It includes information on the state spaces, reward values, and termination criteria that is not included in the official documentation and can be very helpful in setting up your initial analyses of each environment.

More OpenAI Gym environments

OpenAI Gym has modeled a number of classic control theory problems as RL environments, including the inverted pendulum problem we already worked with in CartPole.

We'll go through some of the more popular environments in the next section. Keep in mind that Gym environments have a shared interface that lets you write generalized algorithms that can potentially be used to solve more than one environment.

You can also create your own environments and upload them to Gym if you carry out the full installation. Instructions are available in the Gym documentation.

Pendulum

The pendulum environment implements the classic inverted pendulum swing-up problem in control theory:

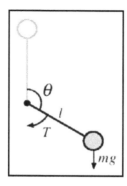

The pendulum is of the length **l** and weight **mg**. It has a rotational velocity and a rotational angle. It is frictionless, and the goal is to keep it pointing upright.

From the preceding diagram, we want to keep the rotational angle theta at zero and the rotational velocity as low as possible. The following is the Gym implementation of the frictionless pendulum:

The pendulum has a random starting velocity and a random starting angle between theta and -theta.

Acrobot

Acrobot is an actuated joint problem first developed by Richard Sutton in 1996:

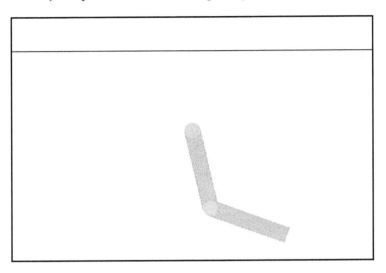

The Acrobot environment is a robot arm that consists of two joints that connect two segments, the top joint rotating from the center of the screen.

The top shoulder joint of the Acrobot is actuated (controlled by a motor that can be rotated in any direction), but the lower elbow joint is unactuated and swings freely. The task is to swing the end of the lower segment to a given height by rotating the top joint.

The Acrobot problem is interesting in robotics and lends itself well to an RL design approach, especially in the design of walking mechanisms, because it requires the controlling mechanism to form a state-space-based understanding of how moving the actuated shoulder joint movement affects the unactuated elbow joint. An RL agent controlling this system would need to model the continuous state space of the system to decide which actions to take from each state (which direction to move the shoulder joint and how hard to swing the arm to get the lower joint to move in the desired direction).

Control theory problems, such as Acrobot and CartPole, are also interesting in the RL space, because a learning agent can approach them without an existing knowledge of the underlying physics or how to model the systems mathematically. They can also be addressed with generalized algorithms that don't take into account the physical specifics of any particular mechanical system. Developing those algorithms to solve these problems allows us to generalize about motion from an RL state-based perspective.

MountainCar

The MountainCar problem has a small vehicle on a one-dimensional path in a valley between two mountains, and its task is to get to the yellow flag at the top of the mountain on the right. MountainCar was first described by Andrew Moore in 1990:

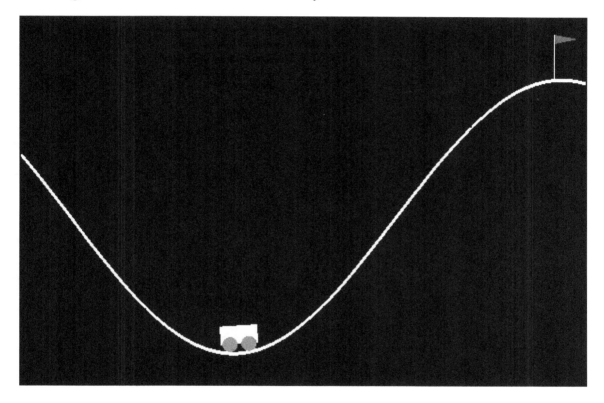

The car's engine is not powerful enough to get it over the mountain peak, so the car has to move back and forth and learn to use momentum to reach the flag. There is a MountainCarContinuous version of the problem that gives a higher reward for spending less energy solving the problem.

Continuous control tasks – MuJoCo

The continuous control series of problems run in a physics simulator called called MuJoCo, which stands for **Mu**lti-**Jo**int dynamics with **Co**ntact. Most of the tasks consist of getting various types of robots to walk or move in complex ways.

HalfCheetah and Humanoid are two of the robots that can be taught to walk or run as part of the MuJoCo continuous control package. A still from the HalfCheetah environment is shown in the following screenshot:

MuJoCo is the first physics simulator designed for use with control-based optimization problems, and it provides consistent generalizations of state spaces in complex simulations of physical systems. A still from the Humanoid environment is shown in the following screenshot:

The best way to get started with the MuJoCo environments is to set one up through the official repository at `https://github.com/openai/gym/tree/master/gym/envs/mujoco/assets`.

You can find the official MuJoCo documentation at `http://mujoco.org/book/modeling.html`.

The documentation provides examples on how to set up an environment and get an agent up and running so that you can start to develop an RL training algorithm.

Continuous control tasks – Box2D

The Box2D set of environments provides more continuous control tasks run with a 2D physics engine. Many of these tasks are based on Atari arcade games, such as Lunar Lander.

Gym also provides a separate library of Atari game-based environments. Lunar Lander is shown in the following screenshot:

The scoring system for the Lunar Lander game, as well as for the other continuous control tasks, is available in the OpenAI Gym documentation and provides the rewards and action spaces, as well as the variables for enumerating the continuous state spaces.

Robotics research and development

Additional Gym environments simulate real-world robotics research projects, such as Fetch and ShadowHand. These robots carry out physical tasks, such as finding and retrieving moving objects and placing them in specified locations. FetchPickAndPlace is shown in the following screenshot:

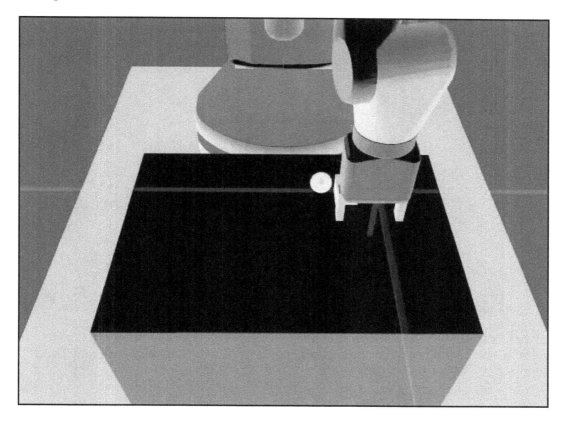

This set of robotics tasks are created to be significantly more difficult than the MuJoCo tasks. All of the environments are goal-based and designed to be solved using continuous state-space RL models.

In FetchPickAndPlace, a goal is randomly chosen in the 3D space, and the objective of the task is to use the robot arm to pick up the red object and put it in the goal. HandManipulateBlock is shown in the following screenshot:

The Fetch and ShadowHand environments have been used to train models that build physical robots. Additional robotics research tasks are continually being designed and added to the Gym package.

Algorithms

The algorithms environments let us train an agent to learn to imitate algorithmic tasks, such as copying characters and adding numbers together. As in any other RL task, the agent is not explicitly told what the task is; it learns through trial and error how to perform the task and when it has performed a correct action:

```
Total length of input instance: 4, step: 3
========================================
Observation Tape  :    DADC
Output Tape       :    DAD
Targets           :    DADC

Current reward    :    1.000
Cumulative reward :    3.000
Action            :    Tuple(move over input: right,
                             write to the output tape: True
                             prediction: D)


 ||   00:43  ━━━━━━━━━━━━━━━━━━━━━━━━━━━━━━━       ↗
                                                  ↙
```

The copy task, shown in the preceding screenshot, involves copying the characters from the observation tape to the output tape.

Regardless of which RL model we choose to solve this or any other task, the model has to learn what the task actually is (Add the following symbols as they appear on the observation tape and moving the cursor to the right after the character is copied).

This is universally true of RL tasks. In environments with discrete state spaces, an agent can take random actions and eventually reach a goal, but an effective RL algorithm will have the agent quickly learning the optimal actions from each state and improve its performance each time. In environments with continuous state spaces, the agent will need a learning algorithm to effectively navigate the state space and solve the task.

Toy text

Toy text environments such as Taxi, which we solved in Chapter 4, *Teaching a Smartcab to Drive Using Q-Learning*, are simple tasks designed to get you started with RL algorithms. Their state spaces are small, discrete, finite, and easily enumerated.

The following is a rendering of the Taxi environment we solved in Chapter 4, *Teaching a Smartcab to Drive Using Q-Learning*. Notice that toy text environments lend themselves to discrete state spaces because the states depend on the positioning of the characters onscreen.

On the other hand, a simulation of a real-world environment, such as in a video game, necessarily has to have a continuous state space because the rendering of the game changes multiple times per second:

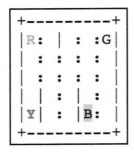

Toy text problems, as we've seen, are relatively easy to solve with a model-free Q-learning implementation, because their state spaces are small and discrete. It's straightforward to construct a lookup table for a small set of state-action pairs.

The FrozenLake environment, for example, contains only 16 distinct states and four actions, as shown in the following diagram:

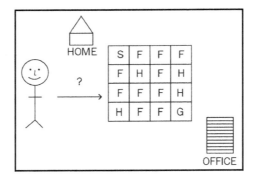

It's only when state spaces become very large that it becomes infeasible to use a simple Q-table. In that case, we try solutions we've discussed such as binning the states, or implementing a neural network or deep learning-based solution to estimate the Q-values.

Contextual bandits and probability distributions

As we saw in the multi-armed previous chapter, the **Multi-Armed Bandit Problem** (**MABP**) can be thought of as lite RL. In the simplest type of problem, we have only actions, rewards, and a probability distribution of reward payouts for each action.

Contextual bandits add a state space or context to the bandit problem, giving us additional information about the environment and providing us with an existing probability distribution for each alternative action we might take, so that we don't have to discover the probability distribution from scratch each time.

Probability and intelligence

What does it mean for an event to have a probability distribution? Where does the probability distribution come from, and what does it tell us about the problem?

Let's first discuss why this question matters. We can classify what we think of as intelligent behavior into two categories:

- Understanding what will happen in the future as a result of your actions and the actions of others (prediction/causality)
- Knowing what actions to take that will get you what you want (decision/utility)

Being able to accurately predict what will happen to you informs your decisions on what you should do to maximize the benefit to yourself. An agent that can do either or both of these things well can be said to behave intelligently.

We make decisions under uncertainty all of the time using our limited existing knowledge of a problem. When our knowledge of the problem increases, we update our model of the problem (our probability distribution of various outcomes). This is what we can refer to, in a general sense, as the learning process.

Updating probability distributions

Think of our probability estimate of an event, such as getting heads when we flip a coin, as what we know about that event. In reality, the event has no probability associated with it. The event will either happen or not. The probability measure exists only in our level of knowledge of the problem:

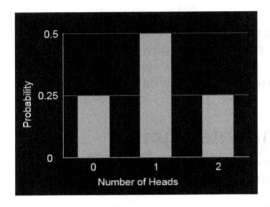

In the preceding diagram, we can see that the probability of getting heads at least once that we observe from flipping a coin twice is 3/4, or 75% (we have a 25% chance of getting zero heads, a 50% chance of getting one, and a 25% chance of getting two).

Our knowledge of the likelihood of getting heads each time continues to change as we flip the coin. We see that the probability curve builds out to a binomial distribution:

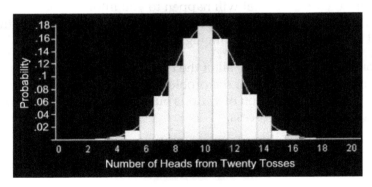

In the case of flipping a coin, if we believe it to be fair, we will guess the likelihood of getting heads on each individual flip to be 50%. If we find, over the course of flipping the coin multiple times, that it might not be fair, or if we find another reason to believe the coin is not fair, we might adjust that likelihood estimate up or down:

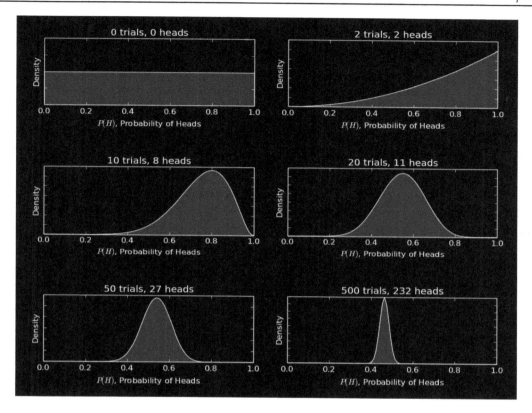

In the preceding diagram, we can see an example of the shifting probability distribution. The more trials we run, the closer we get to the shape of a strict binomial distribution.

We discussed this process earlier in the context of Thompson sampling and the Bayesian control rule, but it's worth exploring further in a more general context.

For a set of events we're investigating, we'll start with a prior distribution of those events, which will be based on the knowledge we currently have. For example, if we have no knowledge of what the actual distribution of an event looks like, we might assume that the distribution is Gaussian (normal or symmetric). As we can see in the preceding diagram, the probability distribution shifts as we conduct more trials and gain more knowledge of the problem.

State spaces

When we are given information about the state of a system, such as a multi-armed bandit environment, the state space becomes part of our knowledge of the problem, and it allows us to adjust our probability expectations of the outcomes we can expect from taking different actions from a particular state.

For example, if we have preliminary information about a potential customer, such as their gender or age, we can take that information into account by incorporating it into the state space when deciding what ads to show them.

In other words, the gender and age of a customer become state variables. As we observe the user behavior of an individual person, we can adjust the state information we have about them to reflect these observations.

The following diagram shows the difference between a typical multi-armed bandit environment and a state-based contextual bandit environment. You will notice that the existence of the state component is the only difference between the two types of problem:

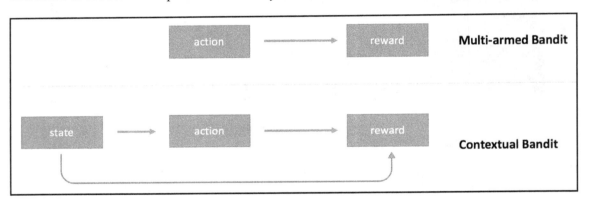

In the MABP, we are attempting not only to learn as much as we can about an environment with incomplete information, but also to benefit from and exploit that environment for the largest gain we can accumulate over time.

We aren't given infinite time to learn an environment, but are continually placed in the position of making decisions with incomplete information and absorbing the consequences of making those decisions. Adding state information to an MABP gives us the information we need to make better decisions about the actions we have available to us than we would otherwise be able to.

A/B testing versus multi-armed bandit testing

One popular application of the MABP is in marketing, where alternative versions of advertisements are shown to users in a process that would normally make use of A/B testing (showing different ads to similar randomly-chosen groups and seeing which one gets the most desired outcomes, such as impressions or clicks):

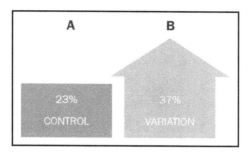

The preceding diagram is a simple illustration of how A/B testing works. One version of an advertisement (or option being tested) whose past performance is known is used as a control, and the other is used as a variation.

The variation is being tested to see whether it will perform better than the control by whatever performance measure is being tested (ad clicks, impressions, or some other metric). If version A (the control) outperforms version B (the variation), version A is kept as a higher-performing option. Otherwise, version B replaces it.

Let's discuss the ways multi-armed bandit testing varies from this approach and the results we can expect to get from each type of experimental trial.

Testing methodologies

Effectively, A/B testing is running a period of pure exploration (using the two options equally to compare their performance), followed by a period of pure exploitation (using the winning option all of the time).

With the multi-armed bandit approach, we are mixing our exploration and our exploitation phases and maximizing our output based on the knowledge we currently have of our action space (the ads we have to choose from).

In other words, we're choosing the best possible option we have now, rather than waiting until the end of the trial to choose the option that won out most often.

The following diagram shows how this works. In A/B testing, we spend half the time doing pure exploration, alternating between A and B (or running them both simultaneously to see their respective success rates). In multi-armed bandit testing, we are using a simple, stateless, epsilon-greedy algorithm to choose the option with the highest Q-value some of the time and a random action the rest of the time:

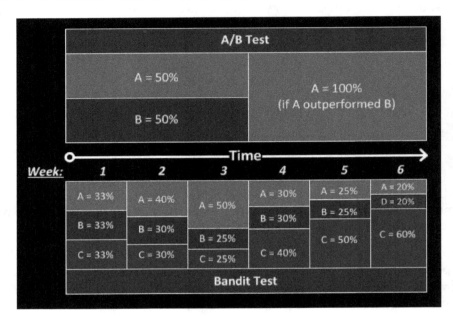

We start the first trial weighting all of the options equally, but by the second trial we are weighting option A more heavily, because it has succeeded more often. We continue this pattern with the third trial. By the fourth trial, we have begun to put more weight on option C, since it is starting to perform better, and so on.

By the sixth trial we've found that option C performs better than the other available options to the point where we're using it in **60%** of trials. We can see that there's a constant trade-off between choosing the option we've currently valued most highly and discovering a new option that might become more valuable.

Summary

Now that we've reached the end of this book, you are in a great position to continue your study of Q-learning with a wealth of knowledge on how to approach RL problems and develop solutions to them as part of the broader community of RL researchers and practitioners. We've provided some additional study resources in the *Further reading* section.

One of the most important things we want to be able to do as RL researchers is track the progress of our own research and compare it to the work of other researchers at other institutions, working under different research methodologies. Tracking progress in RL research is made difficult by the fact that different implementations of environments can lead to large discrepancies in the difficulty level of implementing a solution to an RL task.

As a solution to this discipline-wide problem, OpenAI Gym provides a variety of environments with predetermined state and action spaces to solve the problem of standardizing RL research across the field and develop a consistent set of benchmarks for future RL models.

We discussed a number of these environments and the types of problems they allow us to solve, and how they enable us to create a community of practice around RL research standards. We've also talked about broader problems in RL research and how to improve existing research methodologies using RL.

Questions

1. What is the RL equivalent of a labeled training dataset in supervised learning?
2. What is one of the difficulties of not having a standardized set of environments for developing RL algorithms? How does Gym attempt to solve this problem?
3. What is the difference between an actuated joint and an unactuated joint?
4. What is the benefit of being able to use a single algorithm to solve more than one environment? Explain in two to three sentences.
5. What is the importance of being able to solve generalized control problems in robotics motion?
6. Briefly describe the relationship between a probability distribution and our current estimation of the likelihood of an event.

7. Explain what difference it makes to have a state space available in a contextual bandit problem.

8. Describe the differences in the results of A/B testing versus multi-armed bandit testing in two to three sentences.

Further reading

- *Reinforcement Learning: An Introduction – Sutton and Barto*: `http://incompleteideas.net/book/the-book-2nd.html`

- *Artificial Intelligence: A Modern Approach – Russell and Norvig*: `https://www.cin.ufpe.br/~tfl2/artificial-intelligence-modern-approach.9780131038059.25368.pdf`

- *Playing Atari with Deep Reinforcement Learning – DeepMind Technologies*: `https://arxiv.org/pdf/1312.5602.pdf`

- *Learning to Compose Neural Networks for Question Answering*: `https://arxiv.org/abs/1601.01705`

Assessments

Chapter 1, Brushing Up on Reinforcement Learning Concepts

1. Reward refers to the current point value of taking an action, and value refers to the overall utility of an agent's future actions as a result of taking that action.

2. A hyperparameter value is not determined by anything in the model itself and has to be set externally. Some kinds of hyperparameters might be the depth of or number of leaf nodes on a decision tree model.

3. Because we don't want a learning agent to keep taking the same high-valued actions over and over if there are higher-valued actions available, an exploration strategy has it take a random action with the goal of discovering actions that might be higher-valued than the ones we've already seen. It could be taking a random action as a result of an exploration strategy.

4. In a situation where we would value future rewards more heavily at the beginning of a task, it makes sense to have a higher gamma value at the beginning and reduce it as the task progresses.

5. Q-learning is off-policy, meaning it assumes the agent is following an optimal policy but does not learn what that policy actually is. SARSA is on-policy, meaning it does learn what the agent's policy is and takes actions based on that policy. Practically, this often means that SARSA will take a suboptimal but safer path to the same goal.

6. Q-learning assumes the agent is following the optimal policy. In tasks such as the cliff walking problem, this assumption can often be wrong to the extent that it reduces the performance of Q-learning compared to SARSA.

7. When the agent is following a simple greedy policy, Q-learning and SARSA will produce the same results.

Chapter 2, Getting Started with the Q-Learning Algorithm

1. Generally speaking, a control process is designed to optimize a value or a set of values within a set of limitations.
2. A Markov chain does not incorporate actions or rewards; it only has states and events that will lead from one state to the next.
3. The Markov property is the certainty that knowledge of a system's future states does not depend on knowledge of past states, but only on the current state.
4. The Taxi-v2 environment has 500 states based on the values the state variables can take. State variables are the location of the taxi, the location of the destination, and the location of the passenger.
5. We include these states for simplicity in enumerating the state space. They are unreachable in the task because, in some cases, the environment reaches a terminal state before they can be reached. For example, when the taxi is carrying a passenger and has reached the destination, it cannot travel to any other states because the task is now complete.
6. One programmatic method of discovering hyperparameters is called grid search.
7. We use epsilon to implement the exploration-exploitation process, which causes the agent to take random actions in search of potential reward paths that are higher-valued than the paths it has already seen. We decay epsilon to reduce the amount of exploration the agent carries out as it encounters more of the state space.
8. An alpha value of 1 would be ideal for an environment that is fully deterministic. An alpha value of 0 would cause the agent to learn nothing (the Q-values would not be updated at all).
9. Decaying gamma is effective when you want the agent to focus less on future rewards and more on current rewards as a task progresses.
10. Using the greedy strategy, the agent will always choose the current highest-valued action at each timestep.
11. In some situations, where there is a high cost to taking suboptimal actions, the epsilon-greedy strategy will not perform as well as other strategies.
12. Getting stuck on a local maximum means continually choosing high-valued actions that an agent has already seen at the expense of potentially choosing higher-valued actions that have not yet been encountered. Using an exploration-based strategy is one way to avoid getting stuck on a local maximum.

13. A/B testing is a method of evaluating different versions of an advertising campaign or other hypotheses against each other to compare their performance.

Chapter 3, Setting Up Your First Environment with OpenAI Gym

1. You can do this by cloning the source instead of installing the package from pip. Further instructions are available in the Gym documentation.

2. The term state is commonly used in the terminology of solving Markov decision processes, and the term observation is often used when describing RL environment state spaces. Both terms are equivalent in this context.

3. Calling `env.reset()` resets the environment's state and returns the environment's current observation or state variable.

4. The task will end when the done variable is set to True or the reward is set to 20, depending on your implementation. Both conditions indicate that the task has been solved.

5. Setting env.s will manually change the state of the environment. This is bad practice when implementing an RL strategy; the state should not be set manually when solving a task.

6. A randomly-acting agent does not learn from its actions by keeping track of high-valued paths, so it cannot narrow down the actions it takes as it explores the environment to focus on more valuable actions.

Chapter 4, Teaching a Smartcab to Drive Using Q-Learning

1. The term state is commonly used in the terminology of solving Markov decision processes, and it refers to the same entity as an observation in RL spaces. When describing MDPs specifically, it is consistent with the existing terminology to use the word state.

2. We know the Q-function has converged when updates to the Q-table no longer change its values.

3. The Q-table remains at its current values when the Q-function has converged.

4. When the Q-function has converged, meaning updates to the Q-table no longer cause its values to change, we know that the agent has found the optimal path to the goal.

5. The function `numpy.argmax()` returns the index of the maximum element in an array.

6. The function `numpy.max()` returns the value of the maximum element in an array.

7. The randomly-acting agent cannot learn from its actions. The Q-learning agent is able to tabulate high-valued actions and focus on taking those actions when they have been discovered.

8. In a situation where we are at a higher risk of overfitting as a task progresses, it makes sense to reduce the value of alpha during the course of the task.

9. Overfitting happens when a machine learning model learns overly-specific lessons from the training data it is provided, meaning it performs much better on the training data than on testing data. The alpha hyperparameter is intended to protect an RL agent from overfitting by preventing it from learning from noisy data.

10. The number of required time steps reduces by a factor of at least 10 when the number of training episodes is increased. This may vary based on the design and performance of a particular model.

11. When choosing an action, we select a random number within a specified range. If that number is less than epsilon, we choose a random action, and if it is greater than epsilon, we choose the current highest-valued action.

12. We use a neural network, deep learning architecture, or other function-approximating method when the state space of a problem gets too large to be handled with a lookup table.

Chapter 5, Building Q-Networks with TensorFlow

1. An extensional definition is given in terms of examples. An intensional definition is a dictionary definition, given in terms of a high-level description.

2. Feedforward is the process by which values of individual nodes in a network are calculated, and the values are then multiplied by network weights and used as inputs to other nodes in the next layer of the network.

3. The weights in a neural network are used to calculate values to be propagated through the network. They function as coefficients and are updated through backpropagation to improve the accuracy of the network.

4. Gradient descent is an optimization function that adjusts its parameters iteratively to minimize error. It is used in backpropagation to adjust the weights on a neural network to correctly approximate the desired function.

5. Backpropagation is used to train neural networks by transmitting an error in the network's predictions back to the network weights and using the errors to adjust the values of the weights. This corrective training progressively improves the performance of the network.

6. In policy iteration, the agent's policy function mapping states to actions is represented in the model. In value iterations, the actual Q-values are updated until the function converges, but the agent's policy function is not represented in the model.

7. A tensor is a generalized matrix or array that follows transformational rules that an array does not. Unlike arrays, tensors can keep track of computation graphs and gradients.

8. A placeholder tensor is a tensor variable that will get assigned a value after it is created.

9. The Q-network approximates Q-values, calculates the loss function, and backpropagates the loss through the network to update the weights.

10. A deep Q-network involves a more complex architecture than a neural network, which might comprise as few as two layers.

11. A neural network is usually a simpler structure that can consist of only a few layers, such as an input, hidden, and outer layer. A deep Q-network is a more complex architecture that might involve many network layers in different configurations.

Chapter 6, Digging Deeper into Deep Q-Networks with Keras and TensorFlow

1. Keras abstracts many of the functionalities provided by TensorFlow and creates a high-level frontend for creating complex deep learning architectures.

2. CartPole is effectively a binary prediction problem because there are two options provided for every action taken.

3. When the state space is very large, some states can be grouped together and treated similarly when the optimal actions to take from those states are the same.

4. Experience Replay updates the Q-function using samples of past actions rather than updating it after every action. This helps prevent overfitting by smoothing away outlier actions and having the agent forget previous experiences in favor of new ones.

5. An RL model approximating Q-values does not know what those actual Q-values are and progressively develops estimates for those values. A regular DQN is uses the same weights to estimate the target value and generate the Q-value approximation. For this reason, the target values shift as the estimates shift, thereby creating a moving target.

6. Maximization bias is the process by which an algorithm overestimates both the long-term reward values and the action values of a Q-function.

7. When the Q-network overestimates the value of an action, that action will be chosen at the next timestep and its value will once again be overestimated.

8. When all of the actions that can be taken from a state are harmful or do not provide any benefit, we are better off not evaluating the actions from that state at all. Dueling DQNs give us the ability to speed up training by not calculating the values of actions of states that are identified as not valuable.

Chapter 7, Decoupling Exploration and Exploitation in Multi-Armed Bandits

1. The true probability distribution of an event is the actual likelihood of encountering that event. We discover this distribution through repeated experimental trials.

2. Conducting more trials gives us a better picture of the true probability distribution of a problem. In most problem spaces, conducting 10 trials of an event would not give us sufficient data to develop a detailed model of the event.

3. A small sample size might be biased in a way the experimenter is not aware of, and the descriptive statistics of that sample might not be reflected in a larger sample.

4. Thompson sampling is a Bayesian method for optimization that involves choosing a prior probability distribution for an event and updating that as more information about the event is received. Since it is computationally expensive to try to find the true probability distribution of the event, choosing the optimal action based on an approximated sample distribution can lead to high optimization performance at a relatively low computational cost.

5. Thompson sampling has been rediscovered multiple times since it was first developed in 1933. The Bayesian control rule generalizes Thompson sampling to the use of causal structures and represents causal relationships between events.

6. A/B testing effectively consists of a phase that is all exploration, followed by a phase that is all exploitation when the best-performing variant is discovered. In MAB testing, there is a mix of exploration and exploitation as the model decides on high-valued paths to take early on.

7. It's convenient to set up A/B variants with different versions of advertisements, and they can be tested against each other simultaneously. Another useful example problem would be testing different variants of a consumer product to see which one sells more. This could be done either through real-time tracking or through a long-term simulation of product sales.

Chapter 8, Further Q-Learning Research and Future Projects

1. The RL equivalent of a labeled training dataset is a standardized set of environments used to train models built by different researchers using different algorithms so that the models can be meaningfully compared to each other.

2. As one example, enumerating a different set of states or actions for the same environment can greatly increase the difficulty of solving that environment. Gym simplifies this process by standardizing state and action spaces for all environments and giving researchers a level playing field on which to compare results.

3. The movement of an actuated joint can be controlled, such as by a motor, while an unactuated joint moves freely and is not controlled by an outside source.

4. Being able to find a general solution to a state space that applies to more than one space gives us the experience and potential to find solutions to more generalized RL problems. One of the biggest challenges in AI is being able to generalize over problems from different domains and solve multiple kinds of tasks with a single methodology.

5. As part of the problem of developing general AI, as opposed to algorithms that can only solve specific types of problems, the goal of solving these control problems is to develop an overall methodology that can generalize regarding motion and independently implement the inherent laws of physical systems without having been preprogrammed to do so.

6. Our current estimate of the likelihood of an event is based on what we know about that event, and as we increase our knowledge of the specifics of that event, we refine our estimate of its true probability of occurring. In statistical terms, we are updating our prior probability distribution of the event using additional information to generate a posterior distribution.

7. Having a state space gives us more information about each observation than we would have if we only knew that it is a member of a broader population. The state space is an additional source of information that allows us to refine our probability distribution of the potential outcomes of taking an action.

8. A/B testing effectively consists of a phase that is all exploration, followed by a phase that is all exploitation when the best-performing variant is discovered. There is no real-time optimization of reward gradients. In MAB testing, there is a mix of exploration and exploitation as the model decides on high-valued paths to take early on.

Other Books You May Enjoy

If you enjoyed this book, you may be interested in these other books by Packt:

Hands-On Meta Learning with Python
Sudharsan Ravichandiran

ISBN: 978-1-78953-420-7

- Understand the basics of meta learning methods, algorithms, and types
- Build voice and face recognition models using a siamese network
- Learn the prototypical network along with its variants
- Build relation networks and matching networks from scratch
- Implement MAML and Reptile algorithms from scratch in Python
- Work through imitation learning and adversarial meta learning
- Explore task agnostic meta learning and deep meta learning

Hands-On Transfer Learning with Python
Dipanjan Sarkar, Raghav Bali, Tamoghna Ghosh

ISBN: 978-1-78883-130-7

- Set up your own DL environment with graphics processing unit (GPU) and Cloud support
- Delve into transfer learning principles with ML and DL models
- Explore various DL architectures, including CNN, LSTM, and capsule networks
- Learn about data and network representation and loss functions
- Get to grips with models and strategies in transfer learning
- Walk through potential challenges in building complex transfer learning models from scratch
- Explore real-world research problems related to computer vision and audio analysis
- Understand how transfer learning can be leveraged in NLP

Leave a review - let other readers know what you think

Please share your thoughts on this book with others by leaving a review on the site that you bought it from. If you purchased the book from Amazon, please leave us an honest review on this book's Amazon page. This is vital so that other potential readers can see and use your unbiased opinion to make purchasing decisions, we can understand what our customers think about our products, and our authors can see your feedback on the title that they have worked with Packt to create. It will only take a few minutes of your time, but is valuable to other potential customers, our authors, and Packt. Thank you!

Index

A

A/B testing 180
  about 179
  versus multi-armed bandit testing 179
Acrobot environment 166
actions 16, 18, 19
activation function 103
agent's long-term performance
  epsilon, decaying 92
  model-tuning 88
  models performance measures, comparing with
    statistical performance measures 88, 89
  models, training 90, 92
  tracking 88
agent
  Bellman equations, implementing 79, 80, 82, 83,
    84
  implementing 76, 78
  value function 79
Algorithms environment 172
alpha 22
alpha value
  adding 85
artificial intelligence (AI) 9

B

bandit regret 147
baseline agent
  actions, stepping 66, 68
  baseline models, in Q-learning 71
  creating 66
  in machine learning 71
  in Q-learning 71
  task loop, creating 68, 69, 70
Bayesian control rule 151, 152
Bellman equations 20

C

CartPole-v1
  about 118, 119, 120
  actions 120
  states 120
  task 121, 122
cliff-walking
  problem 27
contextual bandits 148
continuous control tasks 168, 170
control process 33

D

DeepMind 161, 162
deterministic
  versus stochastic environments 22
double-deep Q-network 134, 135
DQN loss
  calculating 133
DQN, for solving CartPole problem
  actions, selecting with epsilon-greedy 125
  alpha 124
  building 123
  DQN class, building 125
  epsilon 124
  gamma 124
  Q-values, updating 126
  running 129
  task loop, running 127, 128

E

epsilon exploration
  versus epsilon exploitation 24
epsilon-greedy selection
  implementing 155
epsilon-greedy

selecting 154
  strategy 145
epsilon
  hyperparameter, tuning 93
experience replay
  about 130
  adding in 130
  implementing 131
  results 132
exploration rate epsilon 24
exploration versus exploitation 25
extensional definition
  versus intensional definitions 101

F

fixed Q-targets 134

G

gamma 23
gradient descent 102
greedy strategy 144

I

inverted pendulum problem 118
iterative probability distributions 141

L

learning agent 74, 76
learning parameters
  about 84
  alpha value, adding 85
  epsilon value, adding 86

M

Markov chains 34, 36
Markov Decision Process (MDP)
  about 13, 31, 38, 39, 56
  control process 33
  demystifying 32
  Markov chains 34, 36
  Markov property 36
  solving, with reinforcement learning (RL) 40
Markov property 37
memorylessness 36

menu item
  adding 86
model-free agent 11
Monte Carlo tree search (MCTS) 27
MountainCar problem 167
multi-armed bandit 25
Multi-Armed Bandit Problem (MABP)
  about 47, 142
  bandit optimization strategies 49, 50
  bandit problem, setting up 47, 49
  other applications 50
  solving, in Python 152
multi-armed bandit strategy
  bandit regret 147
  Epsilon-greedy strategy 145
  greedy strategy 144
  optimal decisions 147
  overview 144
  upper confidence bound 146
  utility functions 147
multi-armed bandit testing
  methodologies, testing 179, 180
  versus A/B testing 179
multi-armed bandit
  applications 157
multi-armed bandits
  bandits with knapsacks 157
  in experimental design 155, 156
  testing process 156, 157
Multi-Joint dynamics with Contact (MuJoCo) 168

N

neural networks, with NumPy
  backpropagation 107, 108
  feedforward 107
  implementing 106
neural networks
  hidden layer 102
  input layer 102
  output layer 102
  overview 100, 101
  perceptron functions 103
  Q-learning 109
  ReLU function 105
NumPy

neural network, implementing 106

O

observation 63
off-policy method 26
on-policy method 26
OpenAI Gym environments
  about 164
  Acrobot environment 166
  Algorithms environment 172
  continuous control tasks 168, 170
  MountainCar problem 167
  Pendulum environment 165
  robotics development 171, 172
  robotics research 171, 172
  toy text 173, 174
OpenAI Gym leaderboard
  reference 164
  used, for tracking scores 164
OpenAI Gym
  about 56, 162, 163
  environment 58
  environment, setting up 60, 61
  setting up 58
  used, for RL research standardization 164
  working with 56
optimal decisions 147

P

Pendulum environment 165
perceptron functions 103
policy 12
policy agents
  versus value agents 109
policy-based algorithm 12
policy-based iteration
  versus value-based iteration 21
probability distributions
  about 140, 141, 175
  iterative probability distributions 141, 142
  updating 176, 177
Python
  multi-armed bandit problem, solving 152

Q

Q-learning agent
  environment 41
  optimization problem, solving 42
  states and actions, in Taxi-v2 42, 43, 44
Q-learning hyperparameters
  about 22
  alpha 22
  epsilon 24
  gamma 23
Q-learning model
  alpha, decaying 46
  epsilon, decaying 45
  fine-tuning 45
  gamma, decaying 46
Q-learning
  about 11, 109, 161, 162
  versus SARSA 26
Q-network
  building 110
  defining 111, 112
  training 112, 113, 114

R

rectified linear unit (ReLU) 104
regret 147
reinforcement learning (RL)
  about 10, 15, 31
  decision-making, process 13
  epsilon decay 24
  key concepts 10, 21
  Q-Learning hyperparameters 22
  research 162, 163
  states and actions 11
  used, for solving Markov Decision Process (MDP) 40
  value-based iteration, versus policy-based iteration 21
  versus supervised learning 14
  versus unsupervised learning 14
ReLU function 105
rewards 16, 18, 19, 20
RL research
  standardization, with OpenAI Gym 164

S

sample two-armed bandit iteration 143, 144
sigmoid function 104
simple bandit problem 142
state diagrams 148
state spaces 178
state-action diagrams 38, 39
state-action-reward-state-action (SARSA)
  about 11, 27
  revisiting 51, 52
  selecting, over -learning 28
  versus Q-learning 26
states 16, 18
step function 103
stochastic environments
  versus deterministic 22
supervised learning
  about 15
  versus reinforcement learning (RL) 14
  versus unsupervised learning 14

T

tanh function 104

target network 134
Taxi-v2 environment
  action, selecting manually 64
  exploring 62
  state space 63
  state, setting 65, 66
  valid actions 63
Temporal Difference (TD) 133
Thompson sampling 149, 150
toy text 173, 174

U

unsupervised learning
  about 15
  versus supervised learning 14
upper confidence bound 146
utility functions 147

V

value agents
  versus policy agents 109
value-based algorithm 12
value-based iteration
  versus policy-based iteration 21

www.ingramcontent.com/pod-product-compliance
Lightning Source LLC
Chambersburg PA
CBHW080526060326
40690CB00022B/5039